100 YEARS OF
GLASGOW'S
AMAZING
CINEMAS

The Mecca Picture House

100 YEARS OF GLASGOW'S AMAZING CINEMAS

BRUCE PETER

Polygon
Edinburgh

First published by
Polygon
22 George Square
Edinburgh

Set in Sabon by Falcon Oast Graphic Art
Wallington, Surrey
Printed and bound in Great Britain by
Cromwell Press, Broughton Gifford, Wiltshire

ISBN 0 7486 6210 3

A CIP record for the title is available

A Day at the Pictures

'When I was twelve I lived in Ibrox but went to school in Paisley, which meant I had to get money each day for my tram fare and school dinner. Occasionally I'd go without my dinner, pocket the money and save it up until I had enough for a day at the pictures. I plunked the school and walked into the city centre, which took about half an hour but saved the tram fare. I made for the St Enoch Picture House in Argyle Street. It opened at 10.30 and for 4d you could stay until 12.30. I was often the first to go in and sat enthralled. When I came out I went to Birrell's sweetie shop and bought my 'dinner and tea', a quarter pound of marzipan dates, a sustaining 5d worth. I walked along Argyle Street to Woolworths and wandered around there for an hour or so. There was a lassie called Nellie who stood and belted out the latest hits - more free entertainment. After that interlude a saunter up to Sauchiehall Street took me to the Salon. I got there as the doors opened at 2.30. As the big picture wasn't quite finished by 4.30 I never saw the end because I had to tear myself away by 4.25 to nip across the street to La Scala where, before 4.30, you could get a seat in the stalls for 5d. Up to six o'clock the music was provided by a pianist; the cinema orchestra didn't appear till the evening. For another two or three hours there was I, lost to the world in the adventures of the silent films. I loved it. A real day at the pictures.'

John Urie, recalling the early twenties.

CONTENTS

Acknowledgements

The research for this book was completed thanks to the generous assistance of a Glenfiddich *Living Scotland Award*.

Many thanks are also given to: Bill Beattie, Marion Beveridge, Patrick Brader, Alex Cameron, Edmund Campbell, Forbes Castell, Cinema Theatre Association, Mr Cummings, Ian Cunningham, Chris Doak, Allen Eyles, John Fairlie, Elizabeth Ferguson, June Forsyth, Ian Gordon and colleagues at the Mitchell Library, Govan Reminiscence Group, James Gracie, Forsyth Hardy, Elain Harwood, Xandra Harper, Janet McBain, Elaine McCarron, Barney McCue, Scott McCutcheon, Robin McSkimming, Liana Marletta, Mecca Bingo staff, Ann Menzies, Ian Miller, Tony Moss, Brian Oakaby, John Peter, Baajie Pickard, The Rev Archie and Mrs Robertson, Gaylie Runciman, Tommy Sinclair, George and Ronald Singleton, Robbie Smith, Springburn Museum, Strathclyde Regional Archives (especially Dr O'Brien), Andrew Stuart, David Trevor Jones, John Urie, Tom Weir, Kevin Wheelan.

Special thanks go to my mother, Ann Glen, for her advice and for making sense of and typing the manuscript, and to Glen Murray for his patience and editorial skills.

Preface

The seed of this book was sown years ago when, as a youngster, I visited the George cinema in Bellshill. The George's towering cream-tiled facade stood out invitingly among the sooty terraces and I loved the cavernous interior with its ornate speaker grilles and coloured cove lighting almost as much as the film we went to see.

Two decades ago there was still a bewildering number of cinemas in the Glasgow area. Many of them were old and a little dilapidated but most were fondly patronised and fulfilled an important social function in the communities they served. Today very few remain.

As a design student at Glasgow School of Art I came to appreciate the architectural and social significance of the city's cinemas. The sight of so many of them boarded up or being torn down made me decide to record as much as I could about them and the dearth of documentation I found when I started investigating the subject confirmed my belief in the necessity for some celebration of cinemas in Glasgow's cityscape and social and cultural life. The centenary of cinema and film in Scotland seemed an appropriate time for that celebration to appear.

When I started the research I had no real idea of what I was letting myself in for. As I pored over large-scale maps, old newspapers and industry journals I came across more and more long forgotten cinemas whose individual histories I then felt obliged to look into. Sadly, in a number of ways this work came too late; many of those who worked in the industry had already died and a lot of material had been destroyed. Nevertheless, I was fortunate to meet with many interesting cinema people and such luminaries as the late George Singleton and Charles Oakley who provided me with a mass of information and a great fund of stories.

In terms of architectural merit cinemas are problematic. In Glasgow, as elsewhere, a significant number were cheaply constructed and lacked much sense of visual integrity or respect for their surroundings. On the other hand, their impact on people's lives was immense. So, while attempting to be a comprehensive record of the city's cinemas this book focuses as much on anecdotal history as on design or other aesthetic considerations.

Glasgow's cinemas reflected the character, social status and culture of the areas in which they were located. For that reason the book is organised area by area taking a roughly clockwise sweep around the city and dealing with individual cinemas in chronological order within that framework. The gazetteer offers a concise factual listing, in alphabetical order (by the original name) of every cinema I could discover to have existed in the city and should prove a useful reference.

Some readers will notice that such well-loved cinemas as the Seamore, Strathclyde, Gaiety, Ardgowan, Rosevale, Carlton, Elder, Gem and Wellington Palace are not illustrated. The photographic record of Glasgow's cinemas is extremely uneven and it is frustrating to learn of the large amount of material which has been lost. One decorating company admitted to throwing out boxloads of professionally taken glass plates of the interiors of every ABC cinema in Scotland. The author would be keen to hear (via the publishers) from anyone who has photographic or documentary material relating to Glasgow's cinemas.

Bruce Peter
May 1996

Introduction

On Tuesday 26 May 1896 Czar Nicholas II of all the Russias was crowned; in the British Empire there was unrest in the Transvaal (a prelude to the Boer War) and a cholera epidemic in Egypt; at home, Queen Victoria was about to start her summer holiday at Balmoral while the proceedings of the General Assembly of the Church of Scotland filled whole pages of the newspapers. In Glasgow, a queue gathered outside the **Ice Skating Palace** in Sauchiehall Street. Mr Arthur Hubner, the manager, was about to make Glasgow history.

Opened only a few weeks earlier in a building known to Glaswegians as the Panorama, the Ice Skating Palace was not doing as well as it might. Hubner had been brought in to try to boost its fortunes. He presented new attractions, including sideshows and novelty acts, some of them involving electricity, the wonder of the day. That morning's papers carried an advertisement for an unusual afternoon programme:

THE SKATING PALACE
MAY 26th 1896

1

TODAY — THE TRIUMPH OF THE AGE

THE CINEMATOGRAPHE — DIRECT FROM LONDON

THE CINEMATOGRAPHE — THE CENTURY'S SENSATION

THE CINEMATOGRAPHE — THE RAGE OF LONDON

THE CINEMATOGRAPHE — SCENES FROM ACTUAL LIFE

The brothers Louis and Auguste Lumière had given the first ever public cinematographe show in Paris on 28 December 1895. In February 1896 they brought the show to the Polytechnic Hall in London's Regent Street and, on 13 April, it made its Scottish debut at the Empire Palace Theatre in Edinburgh. Hubner hoped it would be a big crowd puller in Glasgow. It was the start of something phenomenal!

Until the 1870s cattle grazed in fields around Garnethill. By 1882 the area was sufficiently urban to attract the Diorama, a small theatre showing large canvases of famous myths and historical events. For the 1888 International Exhibition the Diorama was converted into the Panorama, a more advanced type of spectacle in which dramatic paintings on rolls of canvas were wound across a proscenium – a fore-runner of moving pictures on film. A series depicting the Battle of Bannockburn, painted by Professor Fleischer of Munich, was a great favourite and The Battle of Trafalgar, The Battle of Waterloo and The Battle of Omdurman were all major successes; the 1880s equivalent of epic movies.

The Panorama's interior had been used to demonstrate the possibilities of electricity for lighting at the 1888 Exhibition. For film shows electric lighting was preferable to the limelight then used in theatres and as one of the first buildings in Glasgow to have it installed the Panorama had a distinct advantage as a cinema.

The original programme was modest enough, consisting of six, flickery forty-foot reels:

1. *A Skirt Dance*
2. *Westminster*
3. *A Blacksmith's Shop*
4. *Blackfriar's Bridge*
5. *The Arrival of the Calais Express*
6. *The Admiralty Pier, Dover*

It was an odd mixture, as most early film performances were, yet, since most Glaswegians had never seen London, far less the English Channel or the Calais Express, it was not without interest. But, whether due to the Ice Skating Palace's location (it backed onto Garnethill, a Bohemian and not entirely respectable area peripheral to the city centre), to competition from a big socialist rally in George Square, or simply to the fact that most people were at work, Hubner's spectacle did not cause the excitement that might have been expected. The *Glasgow Herald* reviewed the event in a couple of pedestrian sentences, apparently more intrigued by the technicalities than by the content of the films: '. . . the cinematographe . . . may be said to create living moving pictures. It is worked by electrical light and shows pictures at a rate of 900 per minute'. It might have been just another sideshow novelty.

By early 1897 Hubner must have done some market research. He started showing specially made films of local interest. *The Departure of the Columba from Rothesay Pier* honoured the famous Clyde steamer and *The Gordon Highlanders Leaving Maryhill Barracks* doubtless aroused patriotic pride as the kilted soldiers marched (probably at a ridiculous speed) down Maryhill Road. The programme was a triumph for Hubner and ran at the Ice Skating Palace for months. Film shows began to look as though they might have serious business potential and other Glasgow showmen and entrepreneurs were not long in getting in on the act.

Walter Wilson had set up a Kinetoscope in his **Colosseum** Warehouse, a department store in Jamaica Street, during the 1895 Christmas holidays. Invented by Edison in 1891, the Kinetoscope was a simple coin-operated machine which showed a short film. Wilson was an ambitious man with diverse business interests. In addition to owning the Colosseum he was the main supplier of limelight and other equipment to Glasgow theatres and music halls. Never one to miss an opportunity, he was inspired by the popularity of his Kinetoscope, and by Hubner's success, to set up a 500 seat cinema in the Colosseum. He heralded its opening, on 30 November 1896, with newspaper ads proclaiming:

> This extraordinary invention is the marvel of the age. Every picture is full of life. The following realistic scenes may be seen at every exhibition of the Kinematograph – the English Channel at Dover; the Ostend steamer and the Calais mail steamer are seen to sail away until lost in the distance; Scenes of everyday life on the boulevards of Paris; An animated railway station scene; A funny comedy called 'Two Strings To Her Bow'; The Czar in Paris. Admission 3d.

The hesitant were advised, 'if you have not seen the Kinematograph, you are behind the age', a challenge bound to get a response from the venturesome and forward-looking Glaswegians. Although it still relied on Lumière material Wilson's show was a great success.

Enthusiasm for film shows was infectious among all social classes. Film booths at showgrounds multiplied and travelling shows were set up in any available hall. George Singleton (of a famous pioneering cinema family, whose story will be told later) recalls that:

> We would move in and tie up a screen against one wall. The films may have been silent, but nothing else was. The projector was set up in the middle of the audience and it rattled and clanked relentlessly. Those highly flammable nitrate film spools would be lying around on the floor and our customers would just drop their cigarette ends and tap out their pipes among them. It terrifies me to think about it now, but there were few safety regulations in the old days. All the while, I walked around with a tray shouting, 'caramels, chocolates, toffee!' As the film started we'd all be plunged into darkness, there were no dimmers in those days, and my father, who loved music, would be thumping away on the piano at the side. Babies would cry, conversations would continue and those who could read would repeat the captions in loud voices for the benefit of the illiterate and short-sighted around them. When a spool broke, everyone would hiss and stamp their feet.

From 1897 onwards, music halls such as the Coliseum, the magnificent Alhambra (Glasgow's largest theatre) and the venerable Panopticon attracted big audiences by adding picture shows to their variety bills and entertainments. Operations such as Crouch's Wonderland (later the St Enoch Picture Theatre), Hengler's Circus and Bostock's Indoor Zoo and Circus (which later housed the Zoo ElectricTheatre) cashed in on the excitement by including films among their attractions. The better off were attracted to cinematographic presentations of the kind given by the musical suppliers Ewing and McIntosh in the palatial St Andrew's Halls, better known for lavish classical concerts.

Cinema's popularity, and its respectability, were greatly enhanced by Queen Victoria's Diamond Jubilee in 1897. It was a spectacular opportunity for the cinematograph and film of the event became the first newsreel in Britain. It aroused immense interest around the country and, in Glasgow, was shown in no less grand a venue than the Fine Art Institute in Sauchiehall Street.

By 1901 Glasgow's fascination with moving pictures was firmly established. The outstanding attraction at the concert hall at the International Exhibition in Kelvingrove Park that year was a cinema show promoted under the trade name 'Biograph'. Part of its enormous popularity was due to the increasing adventurousness of film-makers. One of the Biograph films was shot amid mountains and lochs from a wagon propelled in front of a locomotive negotiating the curves and viaducts of the West Highland Line and another, of an elephant coming out of its bath, was said to be 'so realistic that, as he came towards the camera and appeared to get bigger and bigger, the spectators screamed with fright'.

With film so popular it was inevitable that film exhibition should develop apace from primitive travelling shows, setting up wherever they could find a suitable space, to technically sophisticated performances in comfortable, efficient venues, many of which were notable examples of a prolific and fascinating architectural genre. In Britain this trend was accelerated by an Act of Parliament. In the early days film shows could be given almost anywhere and there were almost no safety regulations. The risk of fire, in particular, was very high. In 1909 a large number of people were killed when the Bazaar Cinema in Paris burnt down. Public concern about picture house safety mounted and the British Government quickly introduced the Kinematographic Act, which demanded certain basic safety standards such as fireproof projection booths, adequate exits and local authority inspection and licensing of cinema premises. The first generation of properly planned conversions and purpose built cinemas emerged to take account of the new regulations. Soon after the Act was passed there were more than fifty licensed halls in operation (this includes public halls licensed for occasional films shows) and Glasgow's first purpose built cinema, the **Charing Cross Electric Theatre**, opened in Sauchiehall Street on 12 May 1910. From then on competition for the growing and increasingly enthusiastic cinema going public was fierce and it spawned the remarkable number and diversity of cinemas explored in the following chapters. A group of entrepreneurs emerged who between them controlled every aspect of Glasgow's cinema industry and whose story forms a large and fascinating part of its history.

From offices in West Nile Street, Prince Bendon's Bendon Trading Company quickly established itself as Glasgow's main supplier of cinema equipment and Bendon rented films, becoming one of the city's first commercial distributors. He also made and exhibited his own films in a travelling show which started in 1904. He had a passion for

Green's Showground on the Gallowgate around the turn of the century.

motor yachts and speed boats, using one of the latter to shoot film on Loch Lomond.

Ralph Pringle, a showman and entrepreneur, toured his 'North American Animated Cinematograph' around leased halls throughout Britain before settling in Glasgow where he was responsible for some of the earliest 'permanent' cinemas. He rented the Queen's Theatre, a music hall occupying the upper floors of a block in Watson Street, just east of Glasgow Cross, which he opened as **Pringle's Picture Palace** in November 1907 and shortly afterwards he converted the Alexander Assembly Halls in Cowcaddens into the **Bijou Picture Palace**.

The Greens are legendary in Glasgow entertainment. They were a large family of Lancashire showman who, a few years before they entered the cinema business, moved their circus show from their native Wigan to Glasgow in search of better fortune. George Green, the head of the family, was quick to see potential in the fledgling cinema and, in the autumn of 1896, he took a decisive step into that business when he went to London to buy a projector and camera equipment from Friese-Green & Paul, Britain's earliest supplier of cine equipment.

George Green's first film shows were given at his showground on the former site of the Gallowgate Barracks in Glasgow's East End. He

6

built a booth fifty feet long and thirty feet wide into which were crammed 500 customers, most of whom stood. Admission was 1d. Green personally made films of local scenes. 'Come and see yourselves as others see you,' was his slogan. At the same time the family had a travelling 'kinema show' with an ornate, collapsible, 800 seat booth. It cost £8,000 to make and equip (a huge amount of money at the time) and included a steam organ. A traction engine, capable of hauling thirty tons, towed the show around Glasgow and the Clyde valley.

Not to be outdone by Ralph Pringle's Picture Palaces, Green decided to acquire a permanent hall. In 1908 he bought the **Whitevale Theatre**, a 1000 seat music hall in the Gallowgate. The land around the new cinema was used as a park for showmen's caravans and Mrs Green collected a shilling a week for each stance. The family moved into a flat above the Whitevale's pay-box and they were all soon involved in running the company's cinemas.

Building on the success of the Whitevale, George Green opened a chain of '**Picturedromes**' around Glasgow, starting in the Gorbals in March 1911. The Picturedromes, typically, had twin towered, pavilion-like facades and plain rectangular interiors ornamented with simple plaster scrollwork incorporating Art Noveau motifs. Though the reels only lasted a few minutes the programmes were noted for their relatively good picture quality. George himself had a liking for documentaries and films with an educational content.

George Urie Scott was an outstanding entrepreneur who became one of the leading figures in the Glasgow cinema industry. Born in the city in 1882, he started his career apprenticed to a cabinet maker. A small man with red hair and a ruddy complexion, his unassuming manner belied great ambition and energy. He became involved in variety theatres and, before long, had interests in the entertainment business ranging from ballroom dancing (he owned the Dennistoun Palais) to variety (he also owned the Empress and Pavilion Theatres, where he nurtured native talents such as Jack Anthony and Lex McLean). In 1908 he formed Scott's Electric Theatres and the company was soon running seven primitive picture houses in Glasgow, Lanarkshire and the Borders. The first **Scott's Electric Theatre** opened in 1909 in the Annfield Halls in the Gallowgate, competing with Green's Whitevale. By the thirties Scott had launched the Cinema Construction Company, a joint venture with the cinema architects Charles J. McNair and Robert Elder. Before the Second World War they built almost all of what were to become the ABC cinemas in Scotland as well as a number of super cinemas for independent owners. Among their finest were the State cinemas in King's Park and Shettleston. Bob Forsyth, a junior draghtsman in McNair's practice during the thirties remembers:

> Scott would come into our office clutching large scale maps of Glasgow districts where he wanted to develop cinemas. He drew circles showing a one mile radius around the sites and found out how many potential customers he had in the area . . . It was actually Robert Elder, the junior partner, who did most of the design work, especially the interiors, but he was a very shy man who didn't want to take the credit for them. Our proposals were invariably returned by Scott with notes saying 'more seats in balcony please', and I would have to try to squeeze in an extra one or two at the end of the rows.

Scott was a keen photographer and, like many of the early cinema exhibitors, made films of his own, but this never developed commercially. It was shrewd dealing in cinemas and theatres which allowed him to buy a fine motor yacht and Williamswood House, the grand South Side mansion where he spent his last years.

James Joseph Bennell first came to the attention of Scottish audiences as the manager of Sydney Carter's Pictures, a travelling show which visited Aberdeen, Edinburgh and Glasgow in 1906. The Glasgow performances took place in the august setting of the St Andrew's Halls and were so successful that Andrew Freer, the Halls' manager, advised Bennell to find a permanent venue in the city, which he soon did. Bennell's first cinema had an odd background. The temperance movement had long been active in Glasgow, one of their activities being to organise non-alcoholic entertainments including Saturday evenings tea concerts in Good Templars Harmonic Association halls. These harmless amusements were fondly known as 'The Bursts' (everyone in the audience was given an orange and an apple in a paper bag and at a set time all the empty 'pokes' were blown up and burst simultaneously to great cheering and clapping). By the end of the first decade of the century their appeal was waning and they were eventually abandoned, leaving many Good Templars halls unused.

Bennell chose the largest of them, the **Wellington Palace**, in Commercial Road, Gorbals, which, like so many early cinemas, had started life as a music hall. He squeezed a projection room into the rear stalls leaving room for an audience of nearly two thousand. 'Bennell's Brilliants' made a slow start in November 1909 but picked up enormously after an extensive promotional campaign in which whole streets at a time were circulated with smartly produced leaflets. The programme for each week was headed patriotically with the name of a British battleship and the stories of the silent films were outlined enticingly. To boost business families were offered two free passes entitling the bearers to admission if they bought a penny programme.

To Gorbal's children Bennell's BB (Bright and Beautiful) Pictures quickly became an institution and during the Wellington Palace's first months the children probably had as much effect as the leafleting in promoting the shows. Bennell's ebullient personality appealed to children. He was like a friendly uncle who greeted them at the pay-box with a smile and a pat on the head and then stood in front of the screen to teach them the BB song:

> The BB Pictures they're all right,
> Ever beautiful and bright,
> We will sing with all our might
> Go and see them every night!

The jingle could be heard all over the Gorbals. Bennell had an interesting programming philosophy, which no doubt contributed to his success. The pictures shown in the evenings were the same as those shown at the children's matinees; he believed that if a film was not good enough for children it was not good enough for their parents.

In 1908 Richard Vincent Singleton began a travelling cinema show. RV Singleton was a staunch socialist who believed in the self improvement of the working classes. He was a founding member of the Labour Party and a supporter of the Suffragette Movement. His son George was born in a tenement in Bridgeton. Singleton had originally been in the printing business but he was quick to realise the possibilities which cinema offered. His first shows were given in public halls around Lanarkshire and Clydeside. The Glasgow Labour Councillors George Smith and James Welsh were family friends (they gave their first film show in 1910). In the 1930's Smith became Glasgow Corporation's Housing Convenor and it was no surprise that wherever new housing schemes were built, a cinema promoted by Smith and Welsh opened nearby. Smith and Welsh sold out to Singleton in 1951 and James Welsh then became Lord Provost of Glasgow.

The Frutin family were Russian Jews with a background in the theatre trade who emigrated shortly before the revolution. Bernard Frutin and his son Alex became proprietors of the legendary Metropole music hall in Stockwell St. By the mid-thirties they had built up a small chain of suburban cinemas. These all had stages and stars from the

Metropole were dispatched to perform as an added attraction to the films.

The eccentric Yorkshireman, Albert Ernest Pickard, was perhaps the most notorious Glasgow cinema entrepreneur. Pickard had been in the entertainment business for some time before he began presenting cine-variety programmes at the **Panopticon** in the Trongate in 1910. He went on to run a number of unusual cinemas, whose stories appear in the following chapters, but he was well known for other activities too. He probably made most of his money in land speculation, buying and demolishing decaying properties to sell the sites for development. He certainly became very rich, and he liked to display his wealth. He had eight limousines ('one for each day of the week and two for Sunday'), he was the first man in Glasgow to have a private aircraft and, in 1928, he generated a lot of publicity around his purchase at Sotheby's of a Kilmarnock edition of Burns for which he paid £800, an impressive sum then. The book was displayed proudly in the foyer of one of his cinemas.

Mrs Isobel Glen recalls an encounter with the redoubtable Pickard at his office in the Panopticon when she called to complain about derelict houses (owned by Pickard) lowering the tone of a residential district in the West End:

> Pickard was a stocky man dressed in tweeds; jacket, plus-fours and Fair Isle pullover. As we talked, a secretary, not too discreetly hidden behind a frosted glass screen, transcribed our whole conversation. Pickard was a rascal and litigious, but a jovial and well-liked character nonetheless.

Doubtless very astute, it has also been suggested that the roguish Mr Pickard verged on being certifiable. Some of his stunts certainly point in this direction; for example, posters advertising the Panopticon carried the slogans 'A.E. Pickard Unlimited' and, bafflingly, 'A.E. Pickard – The Skinless Sausage'! His bizarre life ended tragically in 1964 when, at the age of 84, he was suffocated by smoke from a fire at his home in Great Western Road.

If Pickard was one of the most kenspeckle figures in Glasgow cinema history, Alexander B. King became one of the most revered and respected. King's role in the development of cinema and film was seminal, not only as a major exhibitor but also as an organiser, lobbyist and diplomat, and not only in Glasgow but in Scotland as a whole.

King was born in 1888 and became involved in the entertainment business at the tender age of twelve. His tremendous energy was apparent even then. Every evening after he finished work with the Clyde Navigation Trust he sold programmes at the Princess Theatre, a music hall in the Gorbals. When the show was over he had to pick up the discarded programmes, dust them off and flatten them out for re-sale. It was a humble start for a man who was to achieve so much.

King was politically and socially astute as well as energetic and as he worked his way upwards in cinema and film distribution management he made many useful connections in the Scottish business community. Between the wars, he was responsible for booking films not only for many of Glasgow's independent cinemas but for private cinemas throughout Scotland. A shrewd negotiator, he often sent un-cooperative film renters away from his office quite belittled by his knack of paring their charges to the bone. He sat on the board of Caledonian Associated Cinemas, at one time Scotland's biggest, and only national, circuit and he was a member of the General Council of the Cinema Exhibitor's Association, chairing their Entertainment Tax Committee which, in the 1935 Budget, was instrumental in securing a remmission in Entertainment Tax for cinema seats costing up to 6d, a great relief to the small independent exhibitors whom King supported enthusiastically. He served as Film Officer for Scotland at the Ministry of Information during the years when it looked as though a Scottish film-making industry might take off. In 1937 he was made a Deputy Lieutenant of the City of Glasgow and was awarded the CBE. Another accolade came in 1944 when he was knighted in recognition of his wartime activities with the Ministry of Information and his support for charitable causes helping the war effort. King was a man of vision and influence throughout his long career. In the fifties, as Vice Chairman of the Scottish Tourist Board (which he remained until his death in 1973), he supervised the worldwide distribution of documentary films about Scotland and, in 1960, he founded Grampian Television, whose chairman he was for eight years.

John Maxwell, a small, near-sighted family solicitor with a partiality for pungent cigars, was not only a powerhouse in Scottish film exhibition but left a lasting impression on the British cinema industry as a whole. Born in Glasgow in 1876, Maxwell was the archetypal canny Scot who knew a potentially lucrative investment when he saw one. He was a shrewd and cultured man, widely read and quick-witted. His legal expertise won him esteem and his partnership in the law firm Maxwell, Hodgson & Company, an authority unequalled in the showman's world that was the early cinema industry.

Maxwell first ventured into that world as partner and legal advisor in a company which hired Pollockshaws Burgh Hall for film shows. By 1912 he had a share in the first **Prince's Cinema** in Springburn and soon acquired an interest in a dozen other cinemas in central Scotland. In 1917 he founded Scottish Cinema and Variety Theatres with an office at 105 St Vincent Street, which was running over twenty cinemas in Glasgow alone before it merged with other Maxwell companies throughout Britain to form Associated British Cinemas (better known as ABC) in 1928. ABC (Scotland) Ltd was run independently of the parent company until the outbreak of the Second World War, by which time the circuit was Britain's largest with 408 cinemas under its control. When it came to be integrated there were a few small problems. Maxwell had installed family and friends in key positions in his original Glasgow circuit and new circuit managers sometimes had difficulty controlling cinemas where staff were guided by family loyalties or where working practices were entrenched. Gordon Coombes, who moved to Scotland in 1951 to run the northern section of ABC, taking a cinema manager to task for the slovenly appearance and surly behaviour of one of his staff, was told: 'I ken fine, but I cannae get rid of him. He's Mrs Maxwell's cousin'.

In addition to his ABC empire Maxwell controlled First National Pathé, which made **Blackmail** (the first talking picture made in Britain, directed by the young Alfred Hitchcock), and owned Waverley Films, Scotland's largest distributor. Controlling distribution as well as exhibition was a boon to Maxwell's business. Since around 1912, film renters had largely been able to dictate the terms of film exhibition, but not to John Maxwell.

Maxwell died in 1940 after a long illness, leaving the film world the legacy of the MGM and Cannon cinema chain, which grew out of ABC.

Glasgow's first post-Kinematograph Act generation of converted and purpose built cinemas were undoubtedly basic, but luxurious 'picture palaces' soon began to appear which could rival the finest anywhere in Europe. **The Picture House** in Sauchiehall Street, after its rebuild in 1912 brought together neo-classical, Regency and Palladian architectural elements and used marble, alabaster, deeply sculpted plaster and carved woodwork in a stylistic feast so grand that it set the tone for the London cinemas to follow. A number of other 'Picture Palaces' appeared, especially in the city centre, between the First World War and the late twenties.

The twenties saw the advent of 'atmospheric' cinemas such as the Toledo at Muirend, the Boulevard in Knightswood and the Orient in the Gallowgate, their auditoria embellished with stucco buildings and their ceilings painted or lit to look like dark, starry skies.

The introduction of sound to movies put a large number of smaller, more primitive picture houses out of business. Talkie apparatus was expensive and the new generation of more comfortable and efficient cinemas that emerged around the same time made the competition tougher than ever. By the late thirties there were sleek tiled 'super' cinemas, boldly outlined at night in vividly coloured neon, on most of the main roads into the city, their advertising hoardings carefully placed to attract the attention of passing tram passengers. A greater contrast to the grimy ashlar-faced tenements whose streetscene they shared would be hard to imagine.

In 1939 Glasgow could boast a staggering 114 picture houses with a total seating capacity in excess of 175,000, more cinema seats per head than any other city in the world. Glaswegians had a love affair with the cinema, going on average 51 times a year, while the rest of Scotland went 35 times and the English a mere 21 (CEA figures). For most Glaswegians there were at least two cinemas within ten minutes walk of home. In some areas rival cinemas stood so close together that children queueing for matinees would be bribed with free sticks of rock by one manager and with free balloons by another. People from every social class and all walks of life went to the cinema, from the smartly-suited men and ladies in fur capes who arrived by automobile to the keelies who rolled up in shoals with two jeely jaurs at sordid halls where the weans were allowed to pee on the floor. Cinemas fulfilled a vital social function. They were great public lounges in which couples courted, friendships were made, gossip was exchanged, fights were fought, babies were born and the elderly passed away. The manager often knew all his regular customers and would take time to chat with patrons and happily arrange special events. In working class areas the local cinema provided warmth, relative comfort and much-needed recreational space, particularly during the depression when taking the family to the pictures was often cheaper than keeping the fire and the lights on at home.

Architecturally, however, cinemas were controversial. Aspiring modernist architects condemned them for their flashy facades, poorly finished rear quarters and lack of sympathy towards the existing townscape and found their gaudiness and blatant self-advertisement distasteful, perhaps not realising that a reticent cinema would be a contradiction in terms. Nevertheless cinema construction helped to keep building and other industries alive through the depression. Firms such as George Urie Scott's Cinema Construction Company, which built most of Glasgow's major suburban picture houses, were substantial employers, as were Templeton's Carpets which supplied the ABC and Green's circuits and decorators such as Cosmos and Guthrie & Wells who specialised in cinema paintwork and other details. Film rental and distribution made a significant contribution to the economy and a big 'super' cinema, such as the Paramount, had a staff of almost 200. There was an enormous amount of activity in the cinema business and something of the glamour of the movie world rubbed off on many aspects of it. Even in the fifties the important cinema owners were such celebrities that, at the annual ball held in the splendid Locarno Ballroom for those working in or associated with the trade, members of the public paid 2/6d just for a place in the balcony from which to watch them at play.

Though never such celebrities, there was a key group of Glasgow architects who specialised in cinema design and who made a major impact with their work in this field. Their eclecticism makes them difficult to categorise. Albert Gardner was one of the most eccentric. His designs range from 'atmospherics' (the Orient in the Gallowgate and the Kelvin in the West End) through the coffin-shaped Kinema in Springburn to the truly monstrous Astoria in Possil. His partner, William Glen, however, was a capable designer who set up his own practice and went on to design over a hundred fine cinemas for ABC throughout Britain. It was only in the thirties that Glasgow firms started to develop identifiable styles. John Fairweather's exteriors were often badly proportioned and poorly detailed, but his enormous Corinthian columned auditoria were suitably monumental. William Beresford Inglis's exuberant 'atmospheric' cinemas, with their rich Andalusian interiors, were unmatched, while James McKissack and McNair & Elder did their best work in the moderne style. In the early thirties McKissack's tiled frontages and unadorned interiors pointed to later developments. His Cosmo was an outstanding example of modern architecture of any kind. McNair and Elder's many bold suburban cinemas were some of the finest public buildings of the interwar years; their curvaceous lines and cove – lit auditoria gave Glaswegians a glimpse of the clean, new approach to design associated with the Empire Exhibition, streamlined trains and ocean liners. The dull, worthy modern buildings of the sixties and seventies were no match.

But the days of glory were not to last. Starting in the late fifties and early sixties cinema attendances began to fall off drastically for a number of reasons. Social habits were changing as people became better off and more mobile. Housing improved enormously and increasing numbers of people had a television in their more spacious and comfortable homes, reducing the incentive to go out for entertainment. In the sixties and seventies large suburban areas of Glasgow were demolished for redevelopment, their populations reduced by big migrations to new housing schemes further out of town, leaving fewer potential customers for those cinemas which avoided the demoliton orders. At the same time Hollywood was no longer making so many of the simple aspirational romances, lavish dramas and fast-shooting Westerns that Glaswegians loved, tending to produce films with a more exclusively adult tone, many of which were X-rated in Britain. The ABC circuit, one of Britain's largest and the most dominant in Glasgow began showing adult certificated films as early as 1952 and their release system meant that every ABC cinema in town could be showing the same programme. Most cinemas, particularly the bigger ones in the suburbs, relied for their success on popular appeal to family audiences which these trends substantially impaired. The image of the picture house as a place to which the whole family could escape, regularly and cheaply, from everyday life to dream a little began to fade.

Throughout the sixties and seventies many cinemas closed and many were demolished. Quite a few found new roles. In February 1962, the giant Astoria at Possil Toll began to host bingo sessions as the Top Rank Club and the die was cast for bingo to become the great preserver of cinema buildings, particularly suburban ones. The majority of Glasgow's surviving cinema buildings are, or were until recently, bingo halls. More than thirty years after the first bingo clubs opened, investment continues be made in this still expanding business, but now with potentially negative consequences for old picture houses. The 'first generation' bingo halls, many of them former Green's, Gaumont or Odeon cinemas, are gradually being replaced by luxurious, purpose built bingo clubs.

Of the 114 cinemas open in Glasgow in 1939, only around forty survive, not one in its original form, and only six still operate as cinemas. The work of Glasgow's best cinema architects can still be seen, but many display the dubious work of 'improvers'; facades defaced by metal sheeting and incongruous signs, false ceilings and subdivided auditoria have displaced the glamorous atmosphere created by bright tiles, exotic plasterwork and spectacular lighting. Perhaps it is unrealistic to expect that more of these exciting buildings could have been preserved unscathed when they relied on such transient materials for their effects. The neglect of the war years, post-war austerity and the harsh Scottish climate all took their toll and when the neon was removed, the exterior soot-stained, the paintwork sullied with tobacco smoke and the upholstery worn, much of the mystique vanished. Windowless, roughcast brick sheds with asbestos roofs were often all that was left.

Happily, the last few years have seen the emergence of a new trend. While the number of cinema buildings in Glasgow continues to decline, in response to a sizeable upturn in cinema attendances the number of screens has risen and continues to do so. There are currently 46 screens in the Glasgow area with the promise of more to come. Most of these are in multiplex cinemas, many of them American owned. Sites at Clydebank and East Kilbride are operated by UCI, an amalgamation of Paramount and Universal Studios with a worldwide chain of cinemas. American ownership has led to concerns about monopoly admission prices and reliance on American films to the detriment of the British film industry but these worries seem insignificant when set against the benefits. The high level of US investment in the British cinema industry has made British multiplexes among the best in the world for comfort, presentation and customer service and exciting new developments are on the way. On the Garden Festival site at Pacific Quays, Glasgow District Council is developing a giant 20 screen complex to be leased to MGM and an IMAX cinema with a massive screen may be built nearby, Odeon Cinemas are to open a 14 screen complex at the city end of Paisley Road West and Warner Brothers and Showcase Cinemas both have plans for multiplexes on the outskirts of the city.

The new generation of multi-screen cinema complexes tend to be in non-residential areas and are reached by car rather than by a ten minute walk from home. Though they are no longer such a part of the community as before they offer a bewildering choice of films in comfortable auditoria with perfect sightlines and excellent sound systems. Even with so many people preferring to watch films at home on video or Sky TV, they are profitable and are spearheading a new era in cinema-going.

As Glasgow moves towards the millenium with an improving cityscape and new confidence cinema looks set to enjoy a renaissance. The centenary of cinema exhibition in Scotland is a fitting time to look back over the first hundred years of Glasgow's amazing cinemas, and to celebrate their contribution to the cityscape and to the city's cultural and social life.

The City Centre

Glasgow's impressive city centre stands on the north bank of the River Clyde. Built on a grid layout, it is widely regarded as the Victorian city par excellence. Towards the end of the nineteenth century its importance and wealth were reflected in grand and lofty municipal buildings, office blocks, department stores and warehouses, mostly of grey, red or yellow sandstone. Gorbals, Hutcheonstown, Anderston, Cowcaddens and Bridgeton districts encircled the city cen-

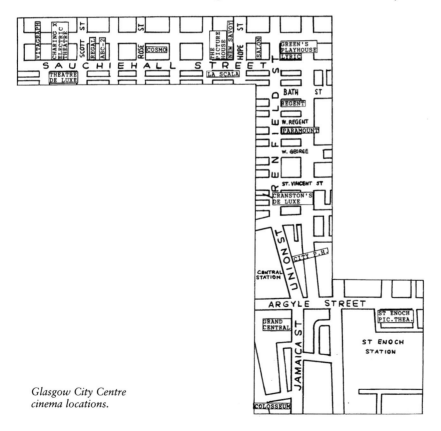

Glasgow City Centre cinema locations.

tre; a belt of over-populated tenement housing interspersed with industry of various kinds. Glasgow had a busy international port and four major railway stations and, by the 1930s, Britain's most extensive tram system transported thousands of people every day from the peripheral districts into the city centre. Nearly every tram route converged on Sauchiehall Street, Argyle Street and the thoroughfare (formed by Jamaica Street, Union Street and Renfield Street) which connects them. These bustling streets were a cinema operator's dream and probably saw more picture houses come and go than any comparable area in Britain.

The First Generation

Due either to the inherent quality of the existing architecture or to native canniness, a number of the early city centre cinemas were built behind existing facades or in converted churches. Following the 1909 Kinematograph Act, several of these appeared on the part of Sauchiehall Street to the east of Charing Cross and on the Argyle Street/Trongate thoroughfare, to be followed by the brand new Cinema Picture House and the splendid little Vitagraph, forerunners

The Charing Cross Electric Theatre. Retaining the existing facade. It was Glasgow's first purpose-built cinema.

of the 'picture palaces'.

Glasgow's earliest purpose built cinema, the **Charing Cross Electric Theatre**, was the first of these and was also innovative in another way. From January 1910 the entertainment columns of the evening papers carried a succinct announcement, 'Kinemacolour coming soon!' and, on 12 May, the Electric opened with this new sensation. The brilliant-white frontage with a concave half-dome above the pay-box blazed with electric light bulbs luring patrons into a stadium-type auditorium which extended into the back court behind. A newspaper report described it as 'a dainty bijou hall decorated in an effective scheme of blue and white' in which patrons could chose between tip-up seats and upholstered benches and where, for a modest 3d, they could enjoy the spectacle of the Wild West, 'real Mexicans and Cowboys and genuine Red Indians with magnificent feathered head-dresses and all the picturesque background and customs of their natural lives'. Kinemacolour involved each frame being painstakingly hand tinted. To audiences used to seeing only black and white films the effect was wonderful and the Electric must have been a place of enchantment. It was enormously popular. Queues stretched for several blocks in both directions and some days after the opening the management had to place a notice in the papers apologising for having to turn away thou-

A.E. Pickard's Panopticon c. 1920. (Strathclyde Regional Archives)

19

sands of would-be customers. But the Charing Cross Electric Theatre was not going to get this enthusiastic audience all to itself. It soon faced stiff competition and, when it closed in 1926, it had been overtaken by progress on many fronts.

A.E. Pickard's **Panopticon** at 115 Trongate was among the competitors. Formerly the Britannia Music Hall, built in 1857, it was already a venerable place of entertainment when Pickard bought it from Arthur Hubner in 1899. Initially Pickard continued to run it as a music hall; the young comedian Stan Jefferson, who became better known as Stan Laurel, cut his teeth in variety there, as did Archie Leach, a dancing stilt walker who later preferred to be known as Cary Grant. To broaden the Panopticon's appeal Pickard added 'an amusement museum, waxworks and fancy fair' and, in 1908, installed a menagerie in the basement which, with great panache, was opened as 'Pickard's Noah's Ark', much to the annoyance of Mr E. H. Bostock, who operated a 'Zoo and Circus' in New City Road in the Cowcaddens.

Pickard started to give cine-variety programmes at the Panopticon in 1910 and these ran successfully until 1926 when the variety was dropped and the Panopticon became the **Tron Cinema**. The name was changed back to Panopticon later the same year (Pickard was prone to sudden changes of mind) but the variety acts were not reinstated and it continued as a cinema until the Second World War. Remarkably, the greater part of the auditorium remains intact, cocooned above a recently opened amusement arcade.

Typical of the first post-Kinematograph Act generation of bigger, better picture houses, the **Argyle Electric Theatre** opened in December 1910. One of many cinemas to take over roller skating halls when the skating craze waned, it was a simple brick building with a fifteen feet wide sliver of vaguely Moorish-looking frontage on Argyle Street. The architect was George Boswell, who abandoned designing church buildings to produce these so-called nickelodeons. In 1938, the original premises were replaced by a stylish new, 1,250 seat cinema just called the **Argyle**. The Argyle became very popular with shoppers and was open from 11am to 11pm every day. It finally closed in March 1960. The Argyle Street railway station now occupies the site.

Also in December 1910, **Dr Ralph Tennyson Jupp**, a London entrepreneur, opened **The Picture House** in a converted furniture store in Sauchiehall Street as one of a chain of cinemas run by his Provincial Cinematograph Theatres Company in the shopping areas of British cities. The furniture warehouse had hosted vaudeville acts and an animated peep show (along the lines of Walter Wilson's Colosseum)

The Argyle Electric Theatre c. 1920. (Strathclyde Regional Archives)

and the original Picture House, like Wilson's, was fairly modest, but it was soon to become one of the most magnificent cinemas in Britain.

King George V and Queen Mary were crowned in 1911, suggesting a name for the cinema which opened in October that year in a former Congregational church at the corner of Dundas and Cathedral Streets. The **Coronation** retained its 1,000 church pews, many of which were at right angles to the screen and there must have been a lot of sore necks as the audience strained to see round the columns supporting the vaulted roof. The Coronation was taken over by new operators in 1912 but only stayed in business until 1915, when the building was demolished.

The **Theatre de Luxe** opened, in November 1911, just across the road from the Charing Cross Electric Theatre and, like it, was squeezed into a shop unit behind an existing facade. An unprepossessing hall with only 262 seats, it succumbed to competition in 1930.

The **Cinema Picture House**, opened in Renfield Street in December 1911, was a forerunner of the 'picture palaces' and successive conversions eventually made it into one. The original grand, regency-style

21

The elegant facade of the Regent after alterations in 1937.

facade was only one storey high and fronted a comfortable, stadium-type auditorium with just over 600 seats. In 1920 it was completely rebuilt. The auditorium was extended along Bath Lane and doubled in height to incorporate a balcony, and a second storey was built onto the facade, retaining all the elements of the original and adding a bay window. It reopened as the **Regent,** the seating capacity more than doubled to 1,314 and Mrs Marion Beveridge, the manager for over thirty years, took great delight in telling English film renters that it had the same number of seats as the year of the Battle of Bannockburn!

In the inter-war years the Regent was a classy cinema with a

The Regent, neon lit, during the 1930s.

The Vitagraph as The King's Cinema during the 1920s. (Strathclyde Regional Archives)

devoted following. It had a solid reputation for thoughtful programming, often sharing the opening of major films with larger venues. After the Second World War it was forced towards the sidelines by the big Odeon and Gaumont houses but it managed to hold its own through the sixties, enjoying some memorable moments, like the visit of the Hollywood star, Danny Kaye, who was hugely popular in Britain. A particularly destructive fire in 1971 almost closed the Regent for good but it was successfully renovated and, despite the proximity of the Odeon, continued to attract loyal customers to its second-run films. Finally closed in 1982, it was torn down to be replaced by an office block called Regent House.

The **Vitagraph**, on Sauchiehall Street just by Charing Cross, opened in 1912 on the site of the premises of the stonemasons who embellished it with the small but delightfully rich facade in Portland stone, with Ionic columns flanked by sculpted torch bearers and surmounted by a large statue of an angel playing pipes. It has an equally magnificent, red sandstone rear facade on Renfrew Street with tall windows and exquisitely carved gargoyles on the pediment above. The deeply recessed Sauchiehall Street entrance led to a vestibule with a pay-box and then up stairs (the steep slope of Garnethill) to a long, narrow auditorium only eight seats wide with a small balcony. Because there was so little space, a back projection system using mirrors was devised. The Vitagraph was an early example of the work of John Fairweather, and the unusual name comes from its own projection equipment.

The Vitagraph was renamed the **King's Cinema** in 1916 and became part of John Maxwell's Scottish Cinema and Variety Theatres circuit when it was founded in 1917. The King's was originally run as an popular upmarket picture house into which a tubby, bearded doorman resplendent in a blue and gold cap, cajoled patrons with a flourish of the folded newspaper he always carried. Many customers still fondly remember the King's from 'the days when the United States Cavalry . . . thundered silently towards you from a mountain pass with 'Old Glory' streaming at their head as they dashed to the rescue of a stockaded fort in the wilderness, the bravery of whose garrison in the face of an Indian attack provided the breathtaking thrills for which you paid . . .' Sometimes, in the early six-reel dramas, fire scenes were tinted red and night scenes blue and the programme was augmented with Pathé's *Gazette* newsreels with their golden-brown, crowing cockerel trademark.

Sadly, the tiny screen and poor quality back projection images eventually relegated the King's to the second rank of city centre cinemas. ABC sold it in 1954 to the London-based Capitol and Provincial Theatres, who renovated and reopened it as the **Newscine**, Glasgow's first cinema to specialise in newsreels, topical films and cartoons. Less than a year later it reverted to normal second-run programmes as the **Newcine**, then, in 1960, a repertory policy was introduced. In 1964, along with Capitol and Provincial's other houses, it was bought by the expanding Classic chain and renamed the **Curzon-Classic**. In the face of declining business it became a strictly members-only Tatler Club in 1973, showing 'uncensored', X-rated films. By 1980, when it became simply the **Curzon**, it was showing Scandinavian soft porn, but this was never a great success and the venerable picture house closed on 22 February 1984 with a double bill of *Loverboy* and *Blood Queen*. It was a nightclub for a while but now lies empty.

The Picture Palaces

In response to the huge popularity of the pictures and to keep ahead in an increasingly competitive market, two sumptuous cinemas appeared in Glasgow in 1912. Among the finest in Britain, they owe much to the tradition of grand, ornate theatres and music halls but begin to look for-

La Scala's auditorium after the 1936 rebuilding.

ward to the super cinemas of the twenties and thirties.

Almost directly opposite The Picture House on Sauchiehall Street, **La Scala** was also a converted warehouse (which explains the excess of windows in the imposing sandstone frontage). Designed by Neill C. Duff and James McKissack as the flagship of the local company, Glasgow Photo Playhouse, its directorate was shared with Glasgow Picturehouse Ltd, which ran the Regent, a ploy to reduce tax liability.

La Scala had a large entrance hall with a carved wooden pay-box, from which a warren of passages and stairways took patrons into an airy rectangular auditorium. A balcony with side slips was supported on columns which undoubtedly spoiled the sight lines for customers in the rear stalls, but The *Glasgow Herald* of 18 October 1912, recording the opening, noted the otherwise excellent appointments:

> At the rear of the central gallery, commanding an excellent view of the screen, boxes have been fitted . . . There are tea rooms and tea lounges both in the area (stalls) and in the gallery (balcony) so situated that patrons can enjoy the entertainment while par-

26

taking of the refreshments.

It was thought romantic to take high tea while watching a film, and the tea-rooms with their shaded lighting soon became popular with courting couples. As *Scottish Country Life* noted in 1928, this feature became the outstanding attraction of La Scala:

> When the theatre was opened, one heard the remark that its catering department would not pay. That prophecy has been entirely falsified as the cafe at La Scala has proved a most popular rendezvous not only with residents in the city but also for their country cousins. It is a decided advantage for busy people to have luncheon or tea and at the same time to see what is being portrayed on the screen . . .

A Christie Unit organ, installed in 1928, was also a great attraction.

La Scala was given a complete overhaul in 1936 to modernise the interior and try to improve the sight lines. Alister G. MacDonald, the son of the Labour Prime Minister, Ramsay MacDonald, was the architect responsible for the attractive results. Warm pink tones with silver details and crimson upholstery were combined with streamline and jazz zig-zag motifs on the side walls and a shimmering silver festoon curtain, lit in red and blue from the footlights, covered the screen.

A highlight of the post-war era at La Scala was the world premiere, on 15 September 1955, of *A Man Called Peter*. Starring Richard Todd and Jean Peters, this story of a Scottish clergyman who became chaplain to the US Senate was slated by the critics as 'dull and worthy', but the launch of an American film in Glasgow was an unusual event.

Always well patronised by an appreciative clientele, La Scala survived the sixties slump and the absorption of the Glasgow Photo Playhouse company into Caledonian Associated Cinemas. In 1976 CAC hacked the lovely interior to pieces in a cheap tripling of the auditorium, but this transformation more than doubled attendance figures and gave La Scala several extra years of profitability. In 1981 it became known as the **Scala Film Centre** and a gold-spangled sign was raised on the facade. Towards the end of its career the Scala was relying on a fraction of ABC's releases and facing stiff competition from newly subdivided rivals with access to better films. In its last years the programmes were mainly horror, 'sexploitation' and repertory and closure came on 28 May 1984. The last audience chortled through *Police Academy* on Screen 1, while *Night Moves* and *Risky Business* appeared on 2 and 3. David Strom, the manager for eight years, observed sadly: 'I'll now be joining the ranks of the unemployed. The last show was just a normal one – the staff didn't think it was a particularly happy thing to celebrate. We just locked the doors and moved off into the night'. A shop now occupies the corner building, and although the cinema interior has completely gone, its original columned entrance has been retained and restored.

Almost exactly two months after the opening of La Scala the lavishly reconstructed **Picture House** opened to great acclaim. Ralph Jupp's Provincial Cinematograph Theatres Company was enhancing its picture houses with improved furnishings and seating and increasing the attraction of going to the pictures by adding orchestras, tea-rooms, lounges and retiring rooms. The new Picture House was one of its finest.

It retained the broad, towering and highly ornate mock-regency, red sandstone frontage, a monumental composition reflecting the wonders within. Film-goers walked through a long colonnade to reach the sumptuous Palm Court, with a fountain, goldfish pool and cages of singing birds, evocatively described in *Scottish Country Life* magazine:

The Palm Court foyer of The Picture House c. 1913.

The Palm Court might have been taken bodily from the palace of some Roman noble of the rich Augustan days. With its lofty marble pillars, spacious staircases and rounded balcony, its regal carved fireplace of white marble, its mosaic floor and garlanded dome, it makes of itself a lovely picture...while the greenery of its palms, the subdued colours of its tapestry panels and the lights gleaming in its silver chandeliers afford further charming features as a setting for the warm kaleidoscope of life and movement in the place.

The auditorium, approached up flights of marble steps, was every bit as opulent. Though narrow and tall by modern standards it was commodious and richly decorated in cream, pale green, lilac and gold with a huge Roman chariot in deeply moulded, gold-painted plaster driving vigorously towards the audience above the proscenium.

The Picture House, with its Wedgewood Room and Oak Room tea lounges, rapidly became one of the most highly praised centres of Glasgow social life. Here at last was a cinema to compete on equal terms with the grandest theatre or music hall. The dignity of the surroundings did not impress everyone though. The marble fountain in the entrance hall proved too much of a temptation for boisterous students who enjoyed throwing one another in, and the water displays were dispensed with when the foyer was extended in 1924. The new attraction was a mighty Wurlitzer organ first played, to a rapturously appreciative audience, on 8 October 1925.

The Provincial Cinematograph Theatres Company was absorbed by Gaumont British in 1928 and The Picture House was renamed Gaumont in 1947. In that year the latest Gaumont Kalee 21 projection equipment was installed and one of the new projectors was proudly displayed in the foyer. The manager proclaimed, 'If it's good enough for the Queen Mary, it'll do for the Gaumont, Glasgow!' By this time Gaumont was part of the Rank organisation and under its ownership the venue continued as a first-run house.

Through the fifties and sixties it launched many new exhibition processes in Glasgow. 3-D, for example, enjoyed considerable popularity when it arrived at the Gaumont on 20 March 1953. A packed house was enthralled by *Bwana Devil* that evening. But 3-D had its problems. The effect required two projectors to be exactly synchronised and thousands of pairs of 3-D glasses had to be cleaned and sterilised after each show. Many youngsters took the glasses home thinking they would make everything 3-D! *The Robe* brought CinemaScope to Glasgow in January 1954, establishing the Gaumont as the city's epic film house. Advance booking began for *The Ten*

The Gaumont's auditorium before the advent of CinemaScope.

Commandments in May 1958 and it ran for four months. *South Pacific*, in Todd-AO, a rival wide-screen format, was an even bigger hit, running for eighteen months in 1958–9, but the Gaumont's biggest success was *The Sound of Music*, screened from 16 April 1965 until 23 December 1967. Projectionist Alex Davidson was reported in a local newspaper as the man who had seen the film over a thousand times. 'Yes, it is a great film,' he agreed, 'but when it opened I did wonder if it would come through the Fair holiday period alright'.

During its later years, the Gaumont was the victim of many destructive alterations. The side wall murals were covered by acoustic tiles and the original proscenium was hidden behind the wide CinemaScope screen which was draped in sickly yellow velour curtains. By the seventies, when wide screen epics films were no longer being made, Rank toyed with plans to subdivide the Gaumont horizontally to be able to show two programmes simultaneously. Instead, closure loomed. The last performance, *Carry On At Your Convenience,* was a pathetic offering for such a grand cinema and the doors closed for the last time on 15 January 1972. A discount shop-

30

The entrance to the Gaumont in 1968.

ping centre now lies behind the still impressive facade.

Mosques, Music Halls and more Warehouses

The appearance of large, luxurious cinemas such as La Scala and The Picture House by no means hindered the building of smaller ones or the conversion into cinemas of assorted premises, large and small. Between the opening of the early picture palaces and the arrival of the first super cinemas in the late twenties, half a dozen new picture houses appeared in Glasgow city centre.

Films had been shown in the **St Enoch Picture Theatre** from 1897 (when it was known as Crouch's Wonderland) as part of variety programmes including 'curios and grotesques'. When it opened under the new name in January 1913 the 'cinematograph' shows were still supplementary to variety and remained so until the old hall (it was originally built in 1881)became a full-time cinema in the late twenties.

31

A rare photo of the Salon, Sauchiehall Street.

The building came under a compulsory purchase order in 1935, but the redevelopment for which the order was issued came to nothing and, almost by accident, it survived. It is currently occupied by a shoe shop, its staid, twin-towered Victorian facade contrasting starkly with the sleek, all-glass St Enoch Shopping Centre next door.

The **Salon**, which opened at 90 Sauchiehall Street in June 1913, was remarkable in a number of ways. It was structurally innovative, being built on ferroconcrete frames, a technique recently developed to give greater resistance to fire. More immediately obvious was its extraordinary exterior which, with a tall frontage clad entirely in brightly-coloured glazed tiles in a flamboyant Moorish style, could easily have been mistaken for a mosque.

The auditorium had a large, comfortable balcony and the considerable space above the cinema was occupied by a luxurious cafe and restaurant two floors high with tiered seating round the upper level. The entire interior of the Salon was bedecked with plaster medallions and scrollwork and the restaurant had an elaborate glazed roof and a wealth of foliage to suggest a winter garden. A lift was installed to encourage patrons to make the long ascent from street level. The newspaper advertisements invited the public to:

Come to the Picture Salon, Winter Garden and Tea Lounge.
Open from 11.30am till 10pm. Specialities – Afternoon Teas and
Teas a la fourchette. Orchestral Music. Comfort and Attention
amid Beautiful Surroundings."

*The Lyric Theatre,
Sauchiehall Street,
seen during World
War I.*

The cinema operation seems quickly to have failed and there is little
information about its later years. Mrs Beveridge, manager of the
Regent, recalls that by 1920 the Salon had become scruffy and outmoded, showing second rate films and said to be frequented by
'women of doubtful reputation.' It closed in May 1923 and, though
the structure remains, none of the Moorish decoration survives.
Behind the current rather nondescript facade, Superdrug occupies the
ground floor, the old cinema is a disco and a Chinese restaurant has
replaced the elegant restaurant and cafe.

In July 1913 the **City Picture House** opened at 60 Union Street. All
that was visible from the street was a narrow entrance, inconspicuous
among the surrounding shops except for the fact that it was flanked
by palm trees in brass bound tubs. The long, irregularly-shaped audi-

torium was a conversion from the City Restaurant and could seat 400.

On the corner of Sauchiehall Street and Renfield Street, the **Lyric** was an interesting if short-lived conversion. A palatial-looking building in French Renaissance style housed shops, offices and a hotel as well as the 2,000 seat theatre, designed by the renowned Frank Matcham and opened as the Royalty in 1879. Cinema shows ran only from 1914 till 1918 when the entire block was purchased by the YMCA. Amateur theatre productions and lectures were given in the Lyric until 1960 when it was sold for redevelopment into a faceless office block called St Andrew's House.

In Jamaica Street the architect W.B. Whittie converted the second and third floors of a fine Venetian style warehouse into the 750 seat **Grand Central**. Opened in August 1915 under private ownership, it became an instant and enduring success. The simply decorated but spacious auditorium had a horseshoe-shaped balcony and its excellent sight lines ensured its popularity. In the early days the Grand Central was upmarket enough to have an orchestra and in the twenties it became the first Glasgow cinema to show De Forest talking films which involved a record being played while the film was running. Great crowds came to see its debut in *Till The Bell Rings*, ironically a satire on the Scottish sabbath.

In the fifties it euphemistically styled itself a specialist art cinema and showed sensationalist continental 'sexploitation' and horror such

The white mass of Cranston's cinema (centre) made an impressive sight at the foot of Renfield Street.

UNION STREET, GLASGOW

as *Les Enfants Terribles, Le Garcon Sauvage* and *Three Forbidden Stories* but when bigger venues began to show this sort of film the Grand Central closed. It lay derelict from 1966 to 1973, when it reopened as the **Classic-Grand**. A new, stalls-only, luxury auditorium with curtained walls and a suspended ceiling was built within the existing shell and initially family-oriented double features were shown. These met with a poor response and the Classic-Grand reverted to its old 'artistic' policy until it was sold again in 1985 and renamed the **Cannon-Grand**. It lingered on until May 1992 when the last lot of lone male customers ascended the potted-plant-lined, dark red stairway to watch a film they would now probably get on video. The auditorium remains unused and is becoming derelict.

In 1916, Miss Catherine Cranston, renowned temperance supporter and proprietor of several Charles Rennie Mackintosh-designed tea-rooms, had an 850 seat cinema installed in the third floor of her latest entertainment complex at the foot of Renfield Street. **Cranston's De Luxe** was built within a particularly well proportioned six storey building with a faience clad facade in Beaux Arts style and Miss Cranston wasted no time in promoting an upmarket image for what was her only cinema. Advertisements declared that 'Cranston's pictures are first run Scotland' (with rival cinemas proliferating, being able to show the latest films first was a great advantage) and 'Cranston's programmes are always the best'. Miss Cranston employed a film advisor to select the pictures. This was none other than James McKissack, the cinema architect, who was by all accounts a kind of latter-day Renaissance man.

After the Second World War, Cranston's was sold to the showman Harry Winocour who quickly re-sold it to the Greens. A newsreel cinema was added in1954, but by this time the Greens were losing interest in cinema operation (like many independent operators they were having difficulty securing the latest releases). The complex was bought by the London-based Classic group in 1960. Classic specialised in repertory cinema and, as it expanded, keenly sought the most profitable programming policies for its houses. In city centres, competition from first run houses, usually meant that this involved 'specialist' programmes – horror, Westerns, cartoons or pornography. Classic tried all four in Glasgow.

In 1969 a third cinema, a Tatler 'members only' club, opened in what had been a billiard room with *I Am A Woman* and *Lust in the Swamps*, and throughout the sixties and seventies the Classic (from 1972 known as the **Classic Film Centre**) ran programmes dominated by horror and low budget erotica. Prim Miss Cranston must have

35

The New Savoy in 1945.

The interior of the New Savoy prior to closure.

36

been turning in her grave. On the night of 22 May 1981 the Classic burned down. The fire-ravaged hulk was used briefly as a performing arts venue and then stood boarded up until 1986 when shops and offices were built behind the original frontage. Restored to its former dazzling white and sympathetically floodlit at night, it is now one of Renfield Street's finest architectural landmarks.

In the same block as The Picture House and less than a hundred metres from La Scala, the **New Savoy** was originally opened in 1911 as a high-class music hall. On Christmas Day 1916 it was reopened as a cinema with the long-forgotten Fanny Ward in a 'sports drama' entitled *A Gutter Magdalene* and *Fairyland*, 'a charming Christmas Phantasy'.

Designed by James Miller, arguably one of Glasgow's best architects of the period, the exterior, if not his best work, was appropriately imposing. The twin-towered frontage was clad in green and grey tiles and a magnificent, if somewhat overwrought, ornamental veranda was cantilevered over the pavement.The interior decoration was carried out exuberantly in Louis XVI style. The spacious vestibule had a comfortable tea lounge (complete with its own 'Roumanian' orchestra) and a stall selling chocolate, cigars and newspapers. Two handsome marble staircases curved upwards to a comfortable waiting room, retiring rooms and, innovatively, a telephone office. The walls were clad in French-polished marquetry panels and mirrors. The auditorium betrayed its theatrical origins with a surfeit of plaster scrollwork, a domed ceiling, boxes with embroidered velvet pelmets and curtains either side of the screen (after 1926 these concealed pipe chambers for a Hilsden organ).

In 1927 the New Savoy became a Gaumont British cinema and, since The Picture House was by then Gaumont's Glasgow flagship, the New Savoy took programmes for their second week. Glaswegians soon learned that films could be seen in the latter 2d cheaper if they were prepared to wait! Although very successful in pre-war years, the New Savoy became an early casualty of the general decline in attendences. By the fifties Rank owned it and, with too many city centre cinemas already, converted it into the Majestic Ballroom. But, with arrival of the disco era, ballroom dancing was also on the wane and the Majestic was closed and demolished in 1972. Rank subsequently developed the Savoy Shopping Centre and disco on the site of what had been both the New Savoy and The Picture House, using the facade of the latter.

Green's Playhouse with its melange of signs and advertisement.

City Centre Supers

By the mid-twenties, inspired by the newest American 'movie-theatres', much larger cinemas were being planned. The 'supers' were on their way. The first generation of Glasgow supers, **Green's Playhouse** and ABC's **Regal**, offered grandeur in traditional style, but the Paramount and particularly the **Cosmo** were architecturally forward-looking as well as luxurious.

Green's Playhouse

It was not one of the big national cinema organisations but a family-owned company which built and operated Glasgow's biggest super cinema. The early exploits of George Green and his sons have already been described. In 1922 they sent the architect John Fairweather to the United States to familiarise himself with the latest cinema design trends. The trip resulted, after four years of construction work, in a 4,368 – seat mammoth cinema on the corner of Renfield Street and West Nile Street. **Green's Playhouse** was a triumph of careful planning; in addition to a cinema it contained offices, tea rooms, a putting range and a ballroom with a reputed maximum capacity of 6,000 dancers. Everything about Green's Playhouse was larger than life; 45 companies were involved in the project, over 16,000 tons of cement were used and special girders and trusses had to be designed to support the double-tiered cinema auditorium and the ballroom above. George Singleton fittingly observed much later that:

> For private individuals to invest so heavily in such a marvellous project, way before the advent of talkies, must have taken great courage indeed. I always admired the Greens for their boldness; their Glasgow Playhouse was a most remarkable theatre.

The construction of the Playhouse was supervised by George Green's sons, Fred and Bert, and was an immense personal achievement for them. The brothers were astute businessmen. Whenever possible they used Green's own employees to do the building work. Clowns, acrobats and showmen, usually employed elsewhere in the company, were taught plumbing, joinery and bricklaying and set to work. The scheme was so carefully budgeted that, to save on travel costs, the workers walked every day from Green's Gallowgate showground to the Renfield Street site and the many outside contractors faced stiff penalties for delayed or unsatisfactory work.

The cinema was opened to great acclaim by Mrs Mason, the Lady Provost, on 15 September 1927 with Monty Banks in *Play Safe* as the main attraction.

Sadly, the Greens did not invest in a new frontage to compliment their epoch-making cinema; the Playhouse was squeezed in between warehouses behind an existing staid stone frontage. But the marquee-style canopy, the big advertising signs and the enormous vertical name sign, lit American-fashion by hundreds of bulbs and with the 'U' of Playhouse mounted crookedly to echo the Greens' advertising slogan

The auditorium seen when new.

'We Want "U" In!' was a spectacular sight at the top of Renfield Street.

Massive staircases and lifts carried patrons to the auditorium, whose main decorative feature was a series of huge Corinthian columns along the side walls interspersed with boxes and supporting hefty cornices. The heavy neo-classical styling was tempered by a bright orange, primrose and gold colour scheme by Guthrie and Wells and by murals designed by John Alexander, a Newcastle-based interior decorator famous for his rich cinema projects. There was a colour change lighting system and the seats were colour coded according to their price. The projection box, crammed into the front of the lower balcony, had refreshment rooms behind it. No space that could make money was unused. Luxury double seats known as 'Golden Divans' were just the thing for courting couples and, ironically, were reputed to give the best view of the screen. In the silent era an orchestra accompanied the shows and the high-kicking Playhouse Dancers performed new routines every week as part of lavish programmes.

Sadly, once talkies came along the Greens found it increasingly diffi-

cult to rent films which would fill the Playhouse; the big film companies were booking the best films for their own cinemas. After the
Second World War the problem became more acute. Films like *The
Jolson Story*, billed as 'the wonder picture' and taking some 400,000
admissions at Green's city centre venues during a three-week run in
February 1947, were few and far between. Throughout the fifties and
sixties Green's cinemas had to rely on the products of minor studios
such as RKO and Republic. When these were taken over by larger studios, the Greens had to make do with re-runs and business began to
fall off badly. The Playhouse cinema closed on 30 June 1973 after a
final performance of *King Boxer*.

While Playhouse cinema audiences declined during the fifties, the
ballroom above was invariably busy, so much so that football turnstiles were fitted to speed up admission! When the ballroom was new,
the licensing authorities doubted that the floor could support the
thousands of dancers expected. Fred and Bert Green had six industrial
concrete mixers hoisted up and invited the press to watch them being
rolled across the Canadian maple dance floor, thus silencing the
doubters. Regularly featuring such famous bands as Joe Loss, the
Squadronaires, Billy Cotton and Doc Crock and his Crackpots, the
Playhouse Ballroom was one of Glasgow's most exciting night-life
attractions and many a romance began there.

Fortunately it was not the end of the line for the building. It was
leased to Unicorn Leisure and refurbished with characteristic seventies
garishness; the entire auditorium was coated in shocking pink with
golden-glitter details which clashed with the new tan, green and
purple seats. New dressing rooms and a £20,000 lighting rig were
installed in readiness for its next incarnation. It was launched as the
Apollo (the name no doubt inspired by the celebrated Harlem theatre
in New York) and Unicorn Leisure promised 'entertainment for all the
family – films and the best in international cabaret', featuring big stars
such as Shirley Bassey and Diana Ross. The Apollo also became
Glasgow's main rock concert venue, a role for which the vast, crudely
tarted up interior seemed to have just the right atmosphere. Many of
the famous names from the rock and pop world appeared and acts
such as The Who, Status Quo, Tina Turner and Paul McCartney filled
the house. Riotous fans often made the huge balcony bounce and
sway alarmingly. The most popular act of all was a local one. Billy
Connolly, banana-booted and unkempt, delivered his *Raw Meat for
the Balcony* to capacity audiences on twelve consecutive nights.
Normally every performer who filled the Apollo got an 'Apollo
Oscar', but Billy was given a miniature silver seat with the attendance

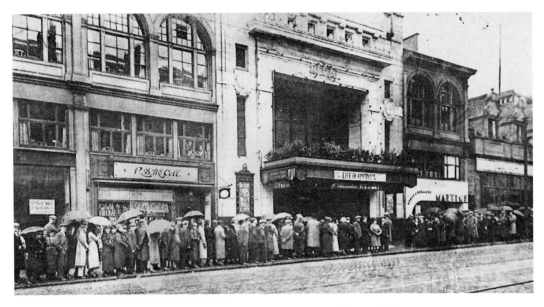

figure stamped on it in recognition of his achievement.

Battered by uproarious rock fans for twelve years, the Apollo finally closed on 16 June 1985 after a concert by Paul Weller and Style Council. When the show ended fans stripped the auditorium of '-souvenirs' and it was boarded up. The old facade was later declared dangerous. The deserted building was broken into and the Ballroom burned down mysteriously in 1987, almost on the eve of its being surveyed with a view to being listed. The demolishers moved in that September and within a few weeks Britain's largest ever cinema was no more.

The Regal

That Green's Playhouse ultimately became a brave but rambling folly was partly due to the arrival of higher quality cinemas with better sightlines and more manageable interiors. In the late twenties, John Maxwell's recently established Associated British Cinemas was looking for a flagship cinema in Glasgow and, fortuitously, bought the former Ice Skating Palace. Since Glasgow's first public cinema show there, the building had been the Hippodrome, a large arena for circus acts with a tank below the ring which could be covered or uncovered whenever a pool was needed. Between 1904 and 1927 this was the permanent home of Hengler's Circus, a well-known Glasgow institution. Hengler's gave film shows full-time between circus seasons. After

Hengler's moved out it became an unsuccessful dance hall called the Waldorf Palais.

The original decoration with 'autumn leaves' murals.

John Maxwell commissioned Charles McNair to convert the structure into a sumptuous super cinema with the latest facilities. The aptly named **Regal** emerged from the partly dismantled shell of the Waldorf Palais and was opened on 13 November 1929 by Lady Weir. 'We should be launching her with champagne,' Maxwell suggested proudly. Invited guests saw, and heard, Al Jolson in *The Singing Fool*, which was something of a sensation but an unusual choice having already enjoyed a record-breaking run at ABC's Coliseum south of the Clyde.

The Regal was a long, three storey building with tall, arched windows framing an assymetrically placed portico clad in cream and black faience tiles and felicitously ornamented with neo-classical and art deco motifs. The site sloped steeply up from Sauchiehall Street so that the auditorium had to be at first floor level with shop units and a car park below. The interior was decorated in autumnal tones and a specially woven carpet with a pattern of interlocking leaves was used throughout. Twin staircases ascended to the stalls foyer from which two storey high windows gave wide views over the street and whose long curtains, potted palms, rattan couches and gilded plaster ceiling

43

The new 1950s décor in the Regal. Bare floorboards in the front stalls give little sense of luxury.

with ornate cornices and chandeliers created a luxurious atmosphere. There was a cafe and smoking lounge either side of the foyer and more flights of stairs led to the upper levels of the auditorium. The auditorium itself was magnificent. A tapering proscenium with ornamental grilles set off illuminated gold screen curtains and on each side wall a *trompe l'oeil* autumnal landscape was viewed between high, pilastered arches which supported an imposing frieze and a lofty, lavishly ornamented, barrel-vaulted ceiling. The army of usherettes, page-boys and ticket checkers were all dressed in the Regal's smart, brown uniform

44

with gold braid and buttons; the usherettes for example, wore a brown tunic and skirt, a black Spanish hat, silk stockings and high-heeled shoes. Every customer was personally shown to their seat.

With the pick of ABC's releases, the Regal was an instant and enduring success with long queues most days. In 1955 a wide screen was fitted and, after the neglect of the war years and the austere post-war period, the opportunity was taken to refurbish the interior. The new side wall treatment was less stately than the original, with plain plasterwork patterned with back-lit recesses, and a fresh pink, turquoise and silver colour scheme brightened the place up.

Such was the Regal's continued popularity that, in October 1967, ABC opened Scotland's first post-war picture house, the unimaginatively named **ABC-2**, next door, renaming the Regal the **ABC-1** at the same time. The 922 seat, stadium-type ABC-2 had an uninspired modernist frontage in brown brickwork relieved only by two rows of small square windows, an upper roof level clad in copper and, on the street, a canopy stretching the full length of the facade. Inside there were a bar and coffee lounges in the foyer and a comfortable semicircular auditorium with an enormous screen covered by wall-to-wall gold curtains.

In 1979, the ABC-1 was closed for quadrupling. The demolition of the once beautiful interior resembled an archaeological dig; the builders kept uncovering evidence of various past uses as they removed layers of plaster and cement. Projectionist Barney McCue recalls that 'when they opened up the floor to build the new supporting frames, they found the old stables and even elephant traps from Hengler's Circus days!' The new five screen complex was inaugurated as the **ABC Film Centre** on 13 December 1979. Compared to the old Regal, the smaller auditoria were almost claustrophobic.

Thorn EMI, who had taken control of ABC, sold it in 1985 to the Australian businessman Alan Bond, of America's Cup fame. Within a week of buying it Bond had resold the company to Messrs Menachem Golan and Yoram Globus, whose production company Cannon, infamous for films such as *The Happy Hooker*, quickly ran into financial difficulties. To survive, Cannon first sold EMI's huge film library to United Artists and then began selling off key cinemas to property developers. Those it retained were renamed **Cannon**. Most of them, including the former Regal, suffered from a crippling lack of expenditure and became very scruffy indeed. A fire, in October 1992, forced its most recent owners, MGM Cinemas, to refurbish the building completely and it reopened in December 1992 as the **MGM**. The renovated Regal frontage is still as impressive as ever and shows up the

The magnificent Paramount at night.

decorative deficiencies of its newer neighbour, the one-time ABC-2. MGM screens 1 and 2 are among the largest in Scotland and the restored foyer still conveys something of the atmosphere of a traditional super cinema.

The Paramount

By the early thirties the *Glasgow Herald* was speculating that Glasgow had reached saturation point with cinemas, but the fact that existing ones were consistently well attended stimulated ever grander schemes.

The American Paramount Corporation commissioned their favourite architects, Frank T. Verity and Samuel Beverly, to design central Glasgow's first entirely new, free-standing cinema, the **Paramount**, which was to be the city's, and Scotland's, most lavish super cinema. Verity and Beverly were highly regarded for their magnificent Italian Renaissance style theatres and cinemas, such as the Paramount in Paris and the Plaza in London, but the new Glasgow Paramount was to be modern.

The first floor of the grand foyer in the Paramount.

The auditorium.

47

A complete block between Renfield Street and West Nile Street was cleared in just seven weeks and a towering facade of cream-coloured reconstructed granite (specially treated to resist urban grime) was built along Renfield Street and curving round the corner into West Regent Street. Above the entrance the sweeping, back-lit canopy was surmounted by five tall windows separated by fin-shaped columns. The most extensive display of neon lighting on any building in Scotland was carried round the facade and along both main street fronts and a six foot high neon name sign in elegant cursive script dominated the skyline. Glasgow had never seen a piece of architecture quite like it.

Inside, the Paramount was even more extraordinary, but before being allowed to discover its splendours customers had to buy their ticket from an external pay-box, an American peculiarity. Passing through the vestibule, they entered a two storey high entrance hall, with a monumental staircase leading to balcony level, whose walls were covered in panels sculpted with a bewildering array of art deco motifs lit from above and below. Throughout the theatre, ceiling coves concealed around 40,000 light bulbs which illuminated the spaces in slowly changing colours. A staff of almost 200 were employed not only see to customer's needs but also to maintain the place!

Upstairs were the Balcony Cafe and Paramount Restaurant. The latter was two floors high and positioned over the main entrance to use the light from the five tall windows in the facade. Rattan chairs, white linen table cloths and swathes of curtaining combined with specially designed carpets, sculpted moderne plasterwork and subdued lighting to splendid effect; the restaurant could have been plucked complete from a trans-Atlantic liner.

The auditorium had 2,784 sprung and upholstered 'theatre chairs' shared between the stalls and the 'Royal Circle' and was decorated in copper, green and silver. An automatic vacuuming system connected to a central cleaning plant 'scientifically cleaned the entire theatre several times a day'. There was a large stage and plenty of dressing rooms for variety programmes. Audiences thrilled to the music of a full orchestra, the strains of a Compton organ with a silver console and the dancing of a troupe of Tiller Girls.

Opened by the Lady Provost, Mrs A.B. Swan, on 31 December 1934, the Paramount immediately became one of the busiest cinemas in Scotland and the most frequented Paramount outside the United States. The manager, Charles R. Young, organised star visits, one of the most popular being the world flyweight boxing champion of 1935,

Benny Lynch. Sporting a bunnet, he was led to the microphone across the huge Paramount stage and, to a standing ovation and prolonged applause, he told the packed audience, 'Tell't yez Ah'd dae it, an' Ah dun it!'

The Odeon in 1966.

Odeon staff pose on the grand staircase, c. 1960.

Opening night of the Odeon Film Centre, 2 October 1970.

Perhaps fearing that Britain would be overrun by German forces, Paramount sold its UK circuit to Oscar Deutsch's Odeon chain in 1939. The acquisition was a major coup, giving Deutsch luxury cinemas in city centre locations, the very thing he had refused to build himself on account of cost. The Glasgow Paramount was shortly renamed **Odeon**. It was subsequently taken over by Rank but kept the Odeon name and throughout all these changes it remained the city's number one picture house.

In the sixties, concerts supplemented films at many of Rank's larger theatres and the Beatles and the Rolling Stones made early appearances at the Glasgow Odeon. Bill Beattie, then an assistant projectionist, has fond memories of these concerts:

> The Beatles came to the Odeon even before they were really famous. I think their last tour date had been in Elgin Town Hall! Anyway, they were real troupers and played to a packed and

50

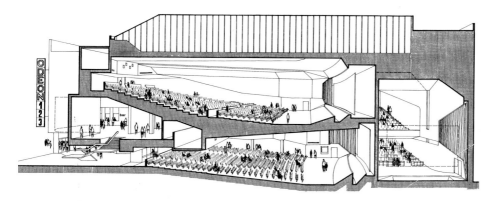

hysterical audience at the Odeon. Roy Orbison once shared the bill with the 'Fab Four' and we could have sold that show for months. The most memorable concert was given by Duke Ellington and his Orchestra in the autumn of 1969. He complained about the cold all day, but gave a terrific show at night, as usual telling the audience that he 'loved them madly' and doing many encores. By then the concerts were making more money than the films.

The arrangement of the Odeon Film Centre.

In 1970, Rank chose to close their other central Glasgow cinemas and concentrate film shows at the Odeon. A comprehensive reconstruction, involving the complete demolition of the existing interior, created three new auditoria. Number 3 was formed out of the stage and backstage areas and, unusually for a multiplex, even had a small balcony. Unlike their gorgeous predecessor, the new Odeons were extremely bland. Painted in unrelieved pale blue, they seemed cold and unwelcoming. But the interior changes were nothing to the indignities heaped on the exterior. The five tall windows and eye-catching fins were unforgivably covered in cheap, grey corrugated sheet metal and a vertical readograph of insensitive proportions was placed centrally above a monstrous new canopy. If the architects intended to completely hide the original grand design, they failed. The additions appear to be just what they are, ugly indiscretions tacked onto the original stonework.

If these efforts destroyed the cinema's aesthetic interest, they did wonders for Rank's profits. In a joint ceremony, the three screens were opened on 2 October 1970 by the triplets Elizabeth, Glenda and Margaret Crammond and, true to previous form, the **Odeon Film Centre** became Britain's busiest cinema. In 1986, screens 2 and 3 were further subdivided to make a six screen complex. Screen 1 was left

51

intact and is now one of the largest Odeon auditoria in Britain. Further attempts at 'improvements' have done nothing to reverse the external damage done in 1970. Perhaps one day Rank will restore to its former glory what is one of Glasgow's best art deco facades.

The Cosmo

The last cinema to be built in central Glasgow before the Second World War did not match the Playhouse, the Regal or the Paramount for grandeur and scale but was perhaps the finest of the lot architecturally.

'Mr Cosmo' – Charles Oakley's cartoon of George Singleton.

Opened on 18 May 1939 as the king-pin of the Singleton circuit, the **Cosmo** was the largest and the only purpose-built 'art' house in Britain outside London's West End. It was devised by George Singleton and Charles Oakley, a Devonian who lectured at Glasgow University. Oakley was a founder member of the Glasgow Film Society (formed in 1928 and thus having a claim to being the world's first) which specialised in screening the foreign films to which he was so devoted. When 'talkies'came along the mainstream cinemas tended to show only English-language films, pushing out even the high quality European ones. The Cosmo, set out to put matters right. The name was derived from 'Cosmopolitan', a small cinema associated with Cambridge University, with which Oakley was familiar. Singleton, whose interest in the venture was more business-like, insisted that a catchy five-letter name was needed.

Designed by James McKissack, whose masterpiece and swansong it was, the Cosmo's geometric, windowless facade was clearly influenced by the Curzon, an upmarket art cinema built in 1934 in Mayfair, London. Both buildings took their inspiration from the designs of the European modernists, particularly from the work of Willem Dudok. As town architect of Hilversum in the Netherlands between 1920 and

*The stylish
Cosmo shortly
after opening.*

1935, Dudok successfully solved the problem of creating visual
integrity in large public buildings. His brick clad structures were conceived as series of massed cubic volumes playing off each other and
were often topped by a central tower feature. His designs were obvious models for cinema architects.

Standing on an awkward sloping site on Rose Street, near busy
Sauchiehall Street, the Cosmo is, nevertheless, undeniably well proportioned. Clad in Ayrshire brick finished with faience cornices,
detailed in cream and amber, and set on a base of black Swedish
granite, the facade of this splendid cinema is as much an expression of
internationalism as the programmes it presents. A small tower above

53

The foyer of the Cosmo.

the entrance creates a monumental impression, while a curve high in the facade reflects the shape of the auditorium within; a rare instance of form following function in a cinema building! As planners insisted that the Cosmo should be set back from the adjacent frontages, a disproportionately large canopy and sign were fitted to advertise the Cinema's presence. The original canopy was golden with neon strip lighting, and the sign cream with red, backlit letters. Sadly the wartime blackout soon extinguished the lights.

The international theme was continued inside, where the two storey high foyer had a globe over the stalls entrance. The vestibule was panelled in walnut. Two suites of offices, including a directors' room, were provided. The neutral and pink toned walls of the streamlined, 850 seat auditorium flowed in a series of subtle curves towards the proscenium and, together with satin curtains and indirect, delicately coloured lighting, created the desired air of seductive sophistication.

Charles Oakley based his programming on that of the Academy cinema in Oxford Street, London, which was regarded as the best art film house in Britain. The Cosmo's opening feature was *Carnet de Bal* (Dance Ticket), starring Raimu, which the management explained would introduce Glaswegian audiences to some of the greatest stars of contemporary French cinema. Special favourites with Cosmo audiences were *Les Enfants du Paradis*, *Fantasia* (a regular at Christmas) and *Jazz on a Summer's Day*, which had queues stretching down

54

Sauchiehall Street.

Despite his intellectualism, Oakley was passionate about cartoons, and these were regularly shown at the Cosmo. He would sometimes phone round the Glasgow cinemas to find where one was playing and, while Cosmo audiences enjoyed a highbrow European movie, he would go off to revel in animated magic at a rival cinema! Quality European films, particularly French ones, were to feature centrally in Cosmo programmes throughout its career, the only exception being during the war years when revivals and run-of-the-mill commercial attractions were shown. 'Entertainment for the discriminating' was the trademark.

On Coronation Day 1953, the events in Westminster Abbey were broadcast live on television and shown to a marvelling Glasgow audience exclusively in the Cosmo. It was the first television performance given in a Glasgow cinema.

Decoratively the Cosmo remained unchanged until 1964, when a small sign appeared on the frontage, in which the 'o's of Cosmo were globes. In 1968, the foyer was remodelled, with a new floor at circle level, and much new wood panelling, in a scheme by Gillespie, Kidd and Coia, the well-known Glasgow architects.

During the sixties, films by such influential directors as Buñuel, Truffaut, Godard and Bergman made their Scottish debuts at the Cosmo and, in 1974 it was bought by the Scottish Film Council to become the **Glasgow Film Theatre**. It was subdivided into a 404 seat cinema in the former balcony and a conference-cum-exhibition space in the stalls. The GFT, as it has come to be known, opened on 2 May 1974 with Frederico Fellini's sophisticated epic *Roma*. Regretably, the original subtle streamlined decoration had been heavily disguised by seventies 'grunge', tartan curtains, orange lights and brown wallpaper. In 1988, a 144 seat cinema replaced the conference room and later a bar (now known as Cafe Cosmo) was added. These new facilities are finished to a high standard and show up the stylistic deficiencies of the seventies alterations.

The Glasgow Film Theatre makes a significant and unique contribution to the cultural life of Glasgow and the West Coast of Scotland. To mark the centenary of cinema in Scotland, a timely programme of restoration is to commence with support from the European Regional Development Fund which will ensure that the GFT continues to be a worthy part of Glasgow's architectural design heritage as well as an important contributor to the city's cultural life.

*The Cosmo's
proscenium with
its decorative
clock and
curtains fitted in
1951.*

The South Side
Gorbals to Rutherglen

The Gorbals

Stretching south behind graceful Carlton Place, which fronts the Clyde, were the grim tenements of 'single ends' (one room dwellings) and 'room and kitchens' and the small industrial premises of the Gorbals.

J.J. Bennel's **Wellington Palace** of 1907 was the area's first full-time, permanent cinema and George Green's first **Picturedrome** of 1911 was not far behind it (see Chapter 1). In 1912, Wee Titch, an infamous Gorbals bookie (nicknamed after a popular music hall star called Little Titch) converted a Free Church building in Cumberland Street into the **Paragon**. Wee Titch intended to operate it himself and had installed a manager called George Archibald, but he sold it immediately to

The Paragon, Gorbals, in the mid 1950s.

Richard Singleton who was keen to get part of the Gorbals cinema business. Richard's son George recalls that Archibald 'left soon after Father bought the place. He became the manager of the New Bedford (see below), went on to become the managing director of Odeon Cinemas and subsequently supervised United Artists' activities in Britain when they took a stake in Odeon in 1940. He ended up as Lord Archibald, a far cry from his early days at the Paragon in the old Gorbals'.

Apart from new external canopies and a projection room, the building was hardly altered from its original use and the dingy interior retained the church pews. George Singleton remembers that 'the patrons were a tough and dirty lot and to maintain cleanliness the place was saturated in carbolic disinfectant', but that the Paragon was 'a good earner. Father and I would fill every last pew'. George did well out of the Paragon even when he parted with it: 'When Oscar Deutsch wanted to expand his Odeon circuit in Scotland, I sold him our chain just before the Second World War. Odeon got the rickety old Paragon and I was able to build some proper super cinemas with the money!'

Though Odeon seems to have been too ashamed of the Paragon to mention it in their group advertising, it continued to make money throughout the war years. After the war things started to go downhill and increasing vandalism and violence came to a tragic head in June 1958 when an elderly doorman was viciously stabbed. The Paragon closed abruptly and was soon demolished.

Like the Paragon, the **Empress** in Ballater Street failed to live up to its grand name. Converted from an old machine shop in 1912, it had no proper foyer or pay-box and seating was on benches in the flat-floored interior. Within three years it was a factory again.

A decorative pediment flanked by gas lamps above a tenement close entrance in Crown Street was the only indication of the presence of the **Crown**, which opened in 1914. The small, gas-lit auditorium with upholstered benches and a tin roof was demolished in 1930 to be replaced by a Lennox and McMath designed, freestanding, jazz moderne, 900 seater, whose rather crude angular facade concealed a bright, comfortable auditorium decorated with zig-zag patterns and sunburst motifs. The Crown was sold to George Palmer's Associated GP Cinemas in 1948 and, following Palmer's usual practice, renamed the **George**. It finally closed in September 1970, a casualty of the depopulation and wholesale destruction of the Gorbals. Most of the Crown Street tenements went with it and monolithic, high-rise blocks fill their place.

The Crown Cinema in 1931.

In 1923 the Paragon and the Crown were joined by a cramped 1,116 seat picture house in Weir Street, Tradeston. The **Ardgowan** was ghastly in every respect. Fashioned out of a defunct cork factory, it was nicknamed 'The Corkie' by the locals and had the usual wooden benches and poor gas illumination of cinemas of its class. Jam jars were standard currency at the Saturday penny matinees and Mrs Jean Melvin remembers the hall full of children eating oranges, a gift from the management, and spitting the pips at each other. The smallest children were singled out as targets and had to take refuge under the benches. The Ardgowan survived until 1963.

During the construction of the Gorbals Street tenements in 1878, a small theatre called Her Majesty's was built between the houses, incorporating the splendid facade (in which five tall windows were separated by six towering Tuscan columns supporting a parapet surmounted by robed figures) from the eighteenth-century, classical-style

*The landmark
frontage of the
Palace.
(Ian Cunningham)*

Virginia Mansion in Ingram Street. In 1904 the massive Palace Music
Hall was built alongside Her Majesty's, cleverly sharing the fine
frontage. The **Palace** was one of the most elaborate examples of the
work of the London-based architect, Bertie Crewe, a rival of Frank
Matcham, and very close to him in spirit. Crewe had trained in Paris
under Vincent Laloux, the designer of the magnificent Quai d'Orsay
railway station and hotel. Standing in humble back courts, the auditorium was wonderfully richly decorated. Stacks of side boxes,
flanked by moulded elephant heads and other fantastic oriental ornamentation, mingled with swirling neo-baroque plasterwork. The
elaborate cornices, columns, niches and statuary were a triumph of the
plasterer's craft.

The Palace introduced cine-variety programmes in 1914 and went
over entirely to cinema in 1930, without significant alteration to its
exuberant interior. It was a cinema until 1962 and then became a
bingo hall. The fact that it was in use got it intact through the redevelopment of the Gorbals, making the demolition, in 1977, of not
only the theatre but also the wonderful facade, all the more

60

unfortunate. Its removal robbed the Gorbals of one of its few remaining landmark structures. Some of the plasterwork from the auditorium was recovered by the People's Palace museum and the statues from the parapet now grace the foyer of the thriving Citizens' (formerly Her Majesty's) Theatre.

The Palace's splendid auditorium prior to demolition.

Eglinton Street

Eglinton Street, the continuation south of the Clyde of Jamaica Street, once boasted three cinemas virtually side by side, two of which still survive as bingo halls next door to one another.

The Eglinton Electreum, opened in 1916, was squeezed into a converted shop and outbuildings. An early cinema design by James McKissack, perhaps influenced by the Mackintosh designed tea-rooms of his friend and sometime employer, Miss Cranston, it was distinguished by an odd, highly-coloured, arcaded street frontage in a debased version of the Glasgow style of art nouveau. The long, narrow and fairly primitive auditorium was entered by a stair leading down beneath the tenements. An Aladdin's cave of delights perhaps; but also a potential fire-trap. Incredibly, the Electreum survived until 1955 and is still remembered by many Gorbals folk.

The original **New Bedford** was a former United Presbyterian Church with an austere, neo-classical frontage. Opened by Wee Titch

61

(of Paragon fame) in 1921, it was sold shortly thereafter to Bernard Frutin. When it was destroyed by fire in March 1932, Frutin commissioned Lennox and McMath to design a replacement, which was opened only nine months later. The second New Bedford, a thirties super constructed to a tight budget, was, stylistically, a development of the Crown, with a rather banally styled, symmetrical, reconstructed-stone frontage dominated by a sunburst mosaic. The 2,300

The second New Bedford in 1934.

seat auditorium was clumsily ornamented with Lennox and McMath's favourite jazz-moderne zig-zags.

In 1936 Frutin sold the New Bedford to the Greens who were looking for a near city centre cinema to complement their gigantic Playhouse. Under Greens' management it continued to show second-run features and in the fifties and sixties, low budget films bought from smaller studios, occasionally sharing the multi-house opening of a big crowd puller. By the seventies the lofty auditorium, cavernous waiting areas and old-fashioned seating were looking dated and worn and competition from more modern cinemas such as the newly tripled Renfield Street Odeon forced it to close. It is now one of Mecca's busiest Glasgow bingo clubs and has recently been refurbished.

The **Coliseum** was designed by the great Frank Matcham, and

63

opened in December 1905 as a music hall by Moss's Empires, Britain's biggest variety circuit. One of Matcham's later designs, the 'Colly', as it was affectionately known, was more restrained than some of his earlier buildings. From the enormous, brick-clad auditorium the narrow entrance facade projected into the street, with, at one end, an octagonal stair tower with a carved stone frieze, and a spire on top. The entrance was through a high archway with tall windows, above which was a loggia under a steeply-pitched pavilion roof. Separate entrances took patrons to each of the three levels of the 2,893 seat auditorium, which was chastely decorated with fine neo-baroque plaster mouldings on the balcony fronts and a splendid marble proscenium arch.

A lively venue throughout its long and varied career, the Coliseum was briefly notorious when, in November 1909, medical students organised a riot to protest against Dr Walford Bodie, a hapless variety artist who performed tricks with electricity. As electricity was becoming more common Bodie's act was wearing pretty thin and the students objected to him calling himself 'Doctor'.

In 1920, after a performance of selections from Wagner, the *Glasgow Herald* claimed that the Coliseum had the best acoustics in the city, a great tribute to Matcham's design principles.

Cine-variety came to the Coliseum in 1925 after it was sold to John Maxwell's Scottish Cinema and Variety Theatres, and, on 7 January 1929, it made Glasgow history when *The Jazz Singer*, starring Al Jolson, became the first talking picture to be shown in the city. Its popularity was legendary. Queues stretched for several blocks and the supporting feature was dropped to fit in more performances. Tram conductors are said to have told their passengers, 'If you want the Coliseum, take the number 8, but if you want the queue, take the number 5'. Women were carried out screaming in distress during Jolson's rendition of the song 'Sonny Boy'; infant mortality was a terrible reality in 1920s Glasgow and for some mothers the intensity of the performance was too much to bear.

Gordon Coombes, who controlled most of ABC's Glasgow cinemas in 1951–52, remembers the special atmosphere at a later stage in the Coliseum's history:

> The vast upper circle was quite phenomenal. To take a walk up there during a house break with the lights on was like visiting another world. Bottles containing suspicious liquids, more likely to be 'wee heavy' than lemonade, were being quaffed. There was much vocal interchange between patrons, generally at the top of

The Coliseum in the early 1960s. (Caledonian Newspapers)

The rear of the Coliseum's huge auditorium betrays its music hall origins. (Scottish Film Archive)

The Jazz-moderne proscenium was built into the former stage area when the Coliseum was renovated in 1931, (Scottish Film Archive)

their voices, and a constant changing of seats to visit friends in different parts of the gallery. Now and again a fight (known as a 'rammy') would develop, but no-one seemed to get seriously hurt. Everybody appeared to accept such carryings-on as a normal part of a visit to the old Colly . . . after all, it only cost ten-pence to get in. By a strange quirk of the acoustics, the more sedate occupants of seats in the stalls and the circle remained oblivious to the noisy proceedings above their heads. . .

In 1962 the Coliseum underwent an ill-conceived, million pound alteration into Scotland's only Cinerama theatre. The auditorium was completely transformed into a 1,310 seat hall with only one balcony below a suspended ceiling and wall-to-wall curtaining hid the gigantic screen. The futuristic new interior was luxurious, but was not a worthy replacement for Matcham's original design. Most unforgivably, a corrugated metal frontispiece was slapped onto the delightful old sandstone facade.

Cinerama was a super-wide screen process using three synchronised projectors to make a vast wrap-around image. The first performance of *How the West Was Won* was warmly received on 26 September 1963 and, perhaps not surprisingly in a tough district like the Gorbals, *The Dirty Dozen* also did well, but Cinerama was not a lasting success in Glasgow. By the seventies Cinerama films were no longer being made and the Coliseum reverted to normal programmes. As a result of the quadrupling of the Sauchiehall Street ABC, that circuit found itself with a surplus of auditoria and the Coliseum closed, with Jack Nicholson in *The Shining*, on 11 October 1980. Glasgow District Council put a compulsory purchase order on the building, with the completion of the Inner Ring Road in mind. Great swathes of the Gorbals were torn down before the road project was abandoned, saving the Coliseum from demolition. The old theatre lay disused until 1987, when it was re-opened (incredibly, since the New Bedford was next door) as a bingo club.

Govanhill and Crosshill

The inaptly named little **Majestic**, opened in Inglefield Street in July 1912, was right at the bottom of the social ladder. Nicknamed 'The Styx', its arched, twin-towered entrance led into a small auditorium which locals remember as badly worn, musty and smelling of urine. But even the smelly Majestic had standards; if you wanted to pay by 'jeely jaur' to watch the Saturday matinee from the wooden benches at the front (two half pound or a single one pound jar covered the penny admission) you had to use the side entrance, while the 'toffs' with cash came in the front. Despite its shortcomings, the Majestic remained open right up till 1957. 'Our Lady of Consolation', a Roman Catholic chapel, now stands in its place.

The early success of his Wellington Palace in the Gorbals led J.J. Bennell to lease the Victoria Road Roller Skating Rink, a massive corrugated iron shed behind a neo-classical facade close to Eglinton Toll, and convert it into the **BB Cinerama.** BB (Bright and Beautiful) came from the Wellington Palace and Cinerama had nothing to do with the wide-screen projection process of the same name. When the Cinerama opened in September 1912 the *Glasgow Herald* praised its appointments: 'A prettily decorated vestibule with tea-rooms on either side gives access to the auditorium, also very effectively designed. Seating accommodation is provided for about 1,500 people and, in respect of heating and ventilation everything has been done for the comfort of visitors.' This was cause for congratulation since conversions of this kind were notoriously uncomfortable.

The first Cinerama was such a success that Bennell opened a new, purpose built one, only a few hundred metres away, in October 1922. The second Cinerama was a stern looking, slightly factory-like, stone-faced, brick building designed by McInnes Gardner. The interior was more welcoming. An oval entrance foyer, panelled in marquetry, led to spacious, comfortable waiting rooms with fluted ceiling light coves

and semi-circular seating niches round the walls, from which grand marble staircases led down to the stalls or up to the balcony. A lift, complete with uniformed lift-man went up to the circle. The auditorium walls were decorated with wooden dados and, between slim pilasters, there were murals of landscaped gardens in various shades of imperial purple. The proscenium was fringed with ornate neo-classical plasterwork.

Mrs Morag Blakeman recalls the Cinerama in the twenties:

> I went with my mother on Friday afternoon. The film was usually a serial. *The Count of Monte Cristo* was my favourite and I wouldn't have missed it for anything. The circle seats cost 9d and free tea and biscuits were served in the interval. They were passed along the aisles by the usherettes and people in the know sat close to the end of the rows to get most of the biscuits.

In 1929 the BB circuit, including the Cinerama, was sold to Gaumont. Part of the deal involved Bennell's son, Ritson Bennell, becoming supervisor of Gaumont's interests in Scotland. A new entrance on Butterbiggins Road, with a leaded glass sunburst above the doors, was added in 1931, but it did little to alleviate the staidness of the building's exterior. J. Arthur Rank's Circuits Management Association Ltd

took over in 1948, changing the name to **New Cinerama** and, in 1964, a complete refurbishment replaced the original decoration with a vulgar mustard, yellow and blue scheme and reduced the seating capacity. It was re-opened as the **Odeon**. By the seventies only the balcony was in use and, in October 1981, with attendances down to as little as twelve a day, Disney's vintage *Snow White and the Seven Dwarfs* was the last show.

The second BB Cinerama as New Cinerama in the 1950s. (Facade to Victoria Road)

Thinking the building had potential as a rock music venue Rank had conversion plans drawn up but, despite the closure of the Apollo in Renfield Street, Glasgow District Council vetoed the scheme and the Odeon was demolished in 1986.

Like their surroundings, Govanhill Cinemas were unpretentious. The **Hampden Picture House** in Westmoreland Street opened in 1920, had bug-resistant, leather tip-up seats and the curtains were still being operated by a man cranking a handle at the side of the proscenium when it closed in 1969. The Hampden's exterior was plain and slightly industrial in tone but had one or two fine scrollwork details and unusual signage with Roman style 'V's for 'U's. It was sold to Greens in 1956. After its closure it was a Mecca bingo club and then a cycling

69

club before its current role as the Clada, an Irish social club, above
whose false ceiling, dim shafts of light filter through ventilators, illu-
minating the simple, barrel-vaulted ceiling and stark side walls of the
slowly decaying old auditorium.

The **Crosshill Picture House** was also opened in 1920, by
J.M. Drummond (the owner of the Crown in the Gorbals). It teetered
on a narrow strip of land above a railway cutting beside Queen's Park
Station. The grand sandstone frontage concealed a ridiculously long
and narrow interior with a cramped balcony. A back-projection system gained the Crosshill a reputation as one of the few cinemas where
the images were less affected by the thick 'pea soup' smogs Glasgow
suffered on still winter days before the Clean Air Act, but otherwise
the awkward shape and lack of facilities were a hindrance to business.
The Crosshill closed in 1952. The building still survives and part of it
is used as a furniture store.

The **Govanhill Picture House** in Bankhall Street, opened in May
1926, was the architectural *pièce de résistance* of the district and its
quasi-Egyptian frontage one of the most eye-catching in Glasgow.
Designed by Eric Sutherland, whose cinema schemes were few and
idiosyncratic, the entrance was decorated with Egyptianesque columns
and stripes of blue and white tiles. A scarab in moulded tiles adorned

70

The Govanhill Picture House in the mid 1960s. (The late Frank Worsdall)

the pediment and the facade was flanked by gold domed towers. An ABC cinema for most of its life, it closed in May 1961, ironically showing *Song Without End*, and soon became one of Glasgow's first bingo clubs. Now a clothing factory, the old Govanhill's sparkling appearance is a credit to its present owners.

The **Calder** was built back to back with the Govanhill and opened in 1932. This handsome little cinema was designed by its builders, Cowiesons Ltd, who gave it a whitewashed, Spanish colonial style frontage capped by a red, pantiled roof. The Calder's programmes were usually serials such as *Tom Mix* or *Flash Gordon*, which ensured the loyal custom of younger audiences every week by leaving the hero in desperate peril at the end of every performance. Greens bought the Calder in 1954 and it showed films until 1967 when bingo claimed it for a short time. It lay derelict for some years before being demolished in 1981.

Battlefield

The **Queen's Cinema** in Battlefield Road, which began its career in 1922, was a good example of how adept early cinema architects were at making the best possible use of difficult sites (which were cheap to acquire). Architect A.V.Gardner manager to squeeze it into the basement and front garden of an awkward, back-to-front tenement block, and its cave-like atmosphere got it nicknamed 'The Catacombs'. It changed hands and was renamed the **Tonic** in 1934. By the fifties, like many other small cinemas, it was having difficulty booking quality commercial films, so the management introduced a continental film policy intended to rival the sophisticated Cosmo in the City Centre. Run by only three staff, a doorman, a manageress-cashier and a projectionist, the little 550 seat Tonic presented European classics such as *Un Grand Patron, Froken Julie* and *Mariage de Figaro* as well as American B-movies. It remained popular as Glasgow's second 'art' cinema until 1962. The building is now a shop.

The **Mayfair** in Sinclair Drive was one of the South Side's best appointed cinemas, but it looked rather odd on the outside. The facade was a *mélange* of facing bricks, roughcast, stained glass and wrought ironwork, the latter having the appearance of an afterthought. It was opened on 1 February 1934 by Baillie John Henderson, who is reported to have talked at excruciating length about the benefits of cinema to tired businessmen and weary housewives, before the tired and weary guests were allowed to enjoy *I Was a Spy*, starring Madeleine Carroll and Conrad Veidt. ABC took over the Mayfair in 1935 and ran it until it closed in 1973. It was a warehouse for a while before being demolished in 1980.

The Mayfair with the distinctive ABC triangle sign prominently displayed. These blue and red logos were fitted to most of the circuit's cinemas after the Second World War. (Ian Cunningham)

Shawlands and Pollokshaws

A comfortably-off area of spacious, high-ceilinged flats in tree-lined streets, Shawlands/Pollokshaws has been well served by cinemas.

The first ones were, as usual, fairly basic. The **Casino** in Shawbridge Street, opened in 1911 and lasted for only four years. Also opened in 1911, the **Camphill** in Baker Street beside Queen's Park, lasted longer, becoming one of Maxwell's SCVT/ABC cinemas in 1929, only two years before it was destroyed by fire. The **Shawlands Picture House** was also owned by ABC. Opened in 1914, it was a nickleodeon-type hall with a corrugated iron roof entered through a close between two shops at Shawlands Cross. The enforcement of licensing regulations closed it in 1930.

The **Maxwell** was a little more interesting, if not much more salubrious. Opened in Shawbridge Street in 1921, its flat-floored, 980 seat auditorium was just a large brick shed, but it had a grandiose, neo-classical frontage. The screen was immediately behind the facade and the main entrance was down a side street. It belonged initially to James Graham, most of whose cinemas were notoriously shoddy. In 1932 it was leased to a J. Boe, renamed the **Palladium,** and its already sordid reputation declined even further till it came to be known as the 'Wee Buggy'. Boe closed it in 1934, claiming to be the victim of flat rate Entertainment Tax, but it was later re-opened by Graham before being sold to a Miss Burns in 1945. Miss Burns gave it a much needed

The Waverley as ABC in 1972. (Ian Cunningham)

73

renovation and it traded successfully as the **Pollok Picture House** until 1958.

None of Shawlands' cinemas quite lived up to the area's middle class respectability until the **Waverley** opened on Christmas Day 1922. Built on a corner at Shawlands Cross to a design by the Glasgow architects Watson, Salmond and Gray (who were to design the Cochrane Street extension to the City Chambers), its weighty, red sandstone exterior, with an imposing dome over the corner entrance, looked more like a burgh hall than a cinema. The interior was rather austere for a cinema of this period and, though it had columns along the sides and a barrel-vaulted ceiling, the rectangular 1,320 seat auditorium was largely unornamented.

On the opening day a big crowd lined Moss Side Road to see the Lord Provost, James Paxton, arrive in his limousine to cut the tape. Paxton was impressed with the Waverley, declaring it a building 'of great dignity which will no doubt effect an outstanding improvement to the amenity of the district'. With good programming and a popular tea-room, the Waverley was a success. In 1928 a Christie organ was fitted, but such instruments went out of fashion after the Second World War and many organists were sacked to save money. The Waverley's organ was removed in 1953. ABC bought the Waverley in 1929 to replace their outmoded Shawlands Picture House, though the name was not changed to **ABC** until 1964. It finally succumbed to bingo in March 1973 and is now a snooker club. The distinctive frontage is listed.

The zany A.E. Pickard opened his largest South Side cinema in Kilmarnock Road in 1927. Part of a complex which contained a dance hall, a restaurant and a car park, it was designed by his friend and 'house architect', H. Barnes, a reclusive and shadowy character whose cinema designs were as quirky as Pickard himself. Pickard held a competition to find a name for the new complex; it ended up being called the **White Elephant** and he had a large model elephant mounted over the entrance. The name was quite appropriate to this cumbersome building with its unusual, 'back-to-front' auditorium entered from below the proscenium. Pickard installed what he called 'lover's neuks', double seats without a central armrest, telling reporters at the opening, 'I didn't like to see young couples doin' their courtin' in closes and I thought it would be better to 'ave them courtin' in my cinema'. 'Winching' was all these seats were good for as they had a fairly restricted view of the screen. In 1934 Pickard sold his cinema circuit to A.B. King, who promptly dropped the 'white' from the name and removed the 'lover's-neuks' (Pickard claimed that 'the new director's

*The Elephant showing an early X-rated film in the mid 1950s. Next week's offering is
Ronald Reagan in Law and Order.*

*The interior of the Elephant with the new CinemaScope screen in 1954. (Strathclyde
Regional Archives)*

wife made a fuss about them'). The **Elephant** was an early casualty of the cinema slump and closed in 1960. The refaced building is now used as shops.

Just a short distance along Kilmarnock Road from the Elephant, the **Embassy** was a real suburban super. Part of Harry Winocour's circuit, it was opened on 3 February 1936 by the legendary music hall star Harry Lauder. The first feature was *Casino de Paris*, starring Ruby Keeler and Al Jolson, a guaranteed success with Glasgow audiences. Designed by James McKissack, the Embassy had an impressive tall facade, with elegant windows flanked by square twin towers, faced in roughcast and detailed in tiles, black up to doortop level and white above. The auditorium had comfortable seating for 1,638. A large stage and dressing rooms perhaps reflected the owners' doubts about the long-term viability of cinema. The Embassy was sold, shortly after it opened, to Glasgow Photo Playhouse (owners of La Scala in Sauchiehall Street) and had a fairly short working life. It was demolished in May 1965 and the site redeveloped as a Shoprite supermarket.

Cathcart

*The Rialto,
Cathcart, c. 1930.
(Tony Moss)*

Cathcart is a comfortable suburb of douce terraced houses with gardens, substantial sandstone tenements and a skyline full of church spires whose citizens first saw Moving Picture shows in the Dixon Halls in Cathcart Road in 1909. The Dixon Halls film shows continued right up until 1938, by which time the **Cathcart Picture House**, the area's first real cinema, had been in business for many years. Built in Old Castle Road in 1913 to plans by the prolific Charles J. McNair, it underwent a major reconstruction (also to McNair's design), before it re-opened as the **Rialto** in November 1928. The Rialto had a curious facade, with rustic roof eaves protruding at the corners, and a balcony, which substantially raised the seating capacity. In 1930 it passed to ABC but, being tucked away in a side street, it had difficulty competing with more prominent rivals and it was sold, in 1948, to George Palmer who, of course, renamed it the **George**. Palmer could not make it succeed either and it stopped showing films in 1961. After a spell of dereliction its temporary salvation came from the Jehovah's Witnesses who made it a Kingdom Hall. It was used for prayer meetings until 1994 when it was demolished to allow a new Kingdom Hall to be

The Kingsway as the Vogue in the 1960s. (The late Frank Worsdall)

built on the site.

The historically more interesting Cathcart **Kingsway** was opened in May 1929 by a company of which James Welsh and George Smith were directors. This fine McKissack cinema had a long, gently curving facade in Spanish-American style. Following the owners' policy of trying to fit as many seats onto a site as possible, the pay-box was placed on the street frontage to save space. The interior, cream, brown and gold and only ornate door architraves continued the Spanish theme. Lion rampant shield motifs on the carpets and screen tabs clashed hopelessly. The Kingsway was sold to the Singletons in 1950 and renamed the **Vogue.** In 1965 the building ceased to be used as a cinema, and for some time housed the Singleton's first venture into bingo. It is now empty and faces an uncertain future.

King's Park

King's Park, to the east of Cathcart, was a massive private housing development, an early thirties bungalow-land first served by the pleasantly named **Florida** cinema in Ardmay Crescent. Built in 1931 to plans by Hamilton Neil for a company in which A.B. King was represented, the Florida was the modernised version of a scheme first proposed by Lennox and McMath two years previously. It had a tall, symmetrical facade; a monumental, red sandstone entrance portico,

The Florida celebrates V.J. Day in 1945. (Kevin Wheelan)

The superb State when new in January 1938. (Strathclyde Regional Archives)

flanked by wings banded in brickwork and roughcast and topped by a red, pantiled roof with prominently projecting eaves. Inside, bright paintwork and coloured lighting created a welcoming atmosphere; sunshine yellow on the ceiling, orange and brown on the beams and pilasters, Wedgewood blue with gilt details on the walls. The auditorium was illuminated by concealed lighting behind imitation windows along the side walls. A tea-room was later fitted into the circle foyer, and hiring this out for functions proved a great success. Lord Provost Sir Thomas Kelly opened the Florida on Hogmanay 1931, when *Cracked Nuts*, starring Woolsy and Wheeler was shown. Seven years later it was sold to **Gaumont** and, in 1949, took that circuit's name. It was demolished in 1962 after lying unused for five years.

The glamourous **State** occupies a prominent site at the crest of a hill on Castlemilk Road. Built for George Urie Scott's Cathcart Picture Playhouse Ltd to an inspired design by McNair and Elder, it had a crisp, streamlined, ultra-modern facade with a bold, vertical name sign. At night the entire building was vividly outlined by red and blue neon strips. The State's foyer had an island pay-box and the large waiting rooms were floored with swirl-patterned terrazzo. In the auditorium, the walls and ceiling curved gently towards the screen, the flowing forms accentuated by parallel slots containing grilles and coloured cove lighting. The State opened on 20 December 1937 with Ruby Keeler and Lee Dixon in *Ready, Willing and Able*. Despite being privately owned and in a relatively thinly populated area, the State stayed in business throughout the difficult sixties. In 1971 the Paulo family bought it and renamed it the **County**, intending to show family films to attract the residents of the vast new Castlemilk council housing development; but films were gradually ousted by bingo which still takes place there. The exterior is now shorn of its important detail but the well kept interior in still a magnificent reminder of the cinema's golden age.

Muirend– *The Toledo*

At Muirend, on Glasgow's southern extremity, William Beresford Inglis built his masterpiece, the superb **Toledo**. A comprehensive essay in his favourite Spanish-American style, it was much more confident and cohesive than any of his previous cinema designs, such as the Arcadia in Bridgeton, the Boulevard in Knightswood or the Ritz in Cambuslang. Externally, the Toledo was a glorious confection of hacienda windows, ornamental balconies and friezes. Inside, the

The Toledo, Muirend in 1934 – a feast of Spanish inspired decoration. (Strathclyde Regional Archives)

Spanish theme was developed into a rich 'atmospheric' treatment.

Although the Toledo was no match for the great American 'atmospheric' cinemas, it was the finest example of the type in Scotland. The original auditorium had a proscenium framed with columns and topped with pantiles. Matadors and butterflies adorned the predominantly red and purple screen curtains. Around the side walls, above exquisitely carved dado panels bordered with jewel-coloured ceramic tiles, whitewashed buildings with red pantiled roofs and balconies mingled with palm trees and amphoras. The ceiling was a dark blue night sky. It cast an enduring spell over its patrons.

The Toledo opened to acclaim on 2 October 1933, but it was sold to ABC almost exactly a year later when Inglis's business ran into financial difficulties. Inglis went on to run the famous Beresford hotel in Sauchiehall Street (the design of which has overtones of a super cinema) and ABC has managed the Toledo ever since, not without incident. In the sixties they proposed converting it into a bowling alley then, in the early seventies, bingo was mooted. Outraged customers collected over 8,000 signatures demanding that it should stay open for film shows and ABC relented, economically tripling the screens in 1981–2. The conversion badly mutilated the original decoration, effectively destroying the interior architectural interest. Screen 3 used video projection, which gave an odd blue cast

81

to the films (it was said to be the only cinema in Glasgow literally showing 'blue' movies) and it was soon abandoned. Muirend was left with two very acceptable cinemas with nearly 900 seats between them. By the late eighties Cannon owned the ABC circuit and was proposing to demolish the cinema to extend the adjacent supermarket car park. The long serving projectionist Tommy Sinclair recalls that:

> These were worrying days for the **Cannon**, as the old Toledo had become known. The company did everything to run the place down. I had to repair the projectors with Sellotape and sticking plaster. For old timers like myself, who took pride in our work, it was very depressing. No wonder I decided to retire and leave them to it . . .

Despite Cannon's attempts to close the place down, patrons remained loyal. Local children petitioned the Secretary of State for Scotland and persuaded him to 'spot list' the worthy building. Though sorely in need of major refurbishment, the last cinema in business on Glasgow's South Side, and one of the few in Britain with 'atmospheric' decor, has hopefully been saved from destruction. Long may it continue!

'Atmospheric' cinemas were an American invention, the undisputed master of the style being John Eberson who, in the 1920s, created fantastic Moorish walled cities, oriental pagodas, Turkish mosques, Gothic castles and neo-classical palaces in three-dimensional plasterwork around the walls of cinema auditoria all over the United States. In most of these the ceiling was a dark blue sky lit by hundreds of twinkling star-like lights and special illumination systems produced changing cloud effects.

Giffnock – *The Tudor*

If the Toledo was an enduring success, the **Tudor** in Giffnock was ultimately a dismal failure. Filling a large corner site on Fenwick Road, it was opened in December 1936 as part of Bernard Frutin's circuit. Designed by Lennox and McMath, the only things about it that could be called 'Tudor' were small wrought ironwork trimmings on the canopy, 'Tudor-bethan' lettering on the name sign and some indifferent murals of scenes from 'Olde England' in the auditorium. These sat incongruously with the simple curving facade and the lavish jazz -moderne decor, with brightly coloured waves and zig-zag patterns

throughout the interior.

Apart from the ample cinema, the Tudor housed a ballroom and a restaurant and, with some foresight, Frutin had bought land across the street for use as a customer car park. The ballroom and restaurant did well, especially when hired out to prosperous parents for children's parties, but the cinema was a disappointment to its owner. People preferred (and could afford) to go into town to see the latest films, while the Tudor had to wait until they had played in Cathcart, Shawlands and Muirend before they finally came to Giffnock. In relatively affluent areas like Giffnock television spread particularly rapidly. Cinemas (and ballrooms) in these areas were very vulnerable to the consequent fall in attendances and it was probably this which finally brought about the Tudor's closure in 1962. Bernard Frutin's son, Alex, sold the property to a group of Jewish businessmen who wanted to build a synagogue but, like so many other cinemas, it was demolished for a more lucrative supermarket development.

The Tudor, Giffnock, in the early 1950s. (Caledonian Newspapers)

Oatlands, Burnside and Rutherglen

On Rutherglen Road, between the Gorbals and the Royal Burgh of Rutherglen, the number 10 tram stopped at Oatlands, where the **Hippodrome** was built in 1921. It was a ponderous, red sandstone building that looked like a bunker, with a small, ornate entrance portico, and a rectangular auditorium, floridly decorated in Louis XV style, with a broken pediment and cartouche above the proscenium. Opened as a variety theatre, it soon began cine-variety; the orchestra accompanied the silent films. From 1925 Bernard Frutin leased the Hippodrome and presented many stars from his famous Metropole, then, in September 1929, sound apparatus was fitted and it became a full-time cinema. Not a great success as such, it was bought in 1931 by ABC, renovated by Charles McNair and renamed the **Ritz**. It was to remain a poor earner, suffering badly from the fact that the best films had been seen everywhere else before they got to the outlying cinemas, and was one of ABC's earliest closures in February 1961. It was later pulled down to make way for a housing development.

In Stonelaw Road, Burnside, Neil C. Duff opened the **Rhul** in 1932. A tall building with a hint of Hispanic styling, it stood out in the suburban street and, by all accounts, was very comfortably appointed. But Burnside, though relatively prosperous, was thinly populated and, the Rhul only got pictures towards the end of their runs. Business was invariably quiet and Duff sold the Rhul, less than four years after its completion, to ABC, who kept it going until 1960, when it was demolished to make way for a supermarket.

In Rutherglen itself, the first film shows were given in the Town Hall as early as February 1897. They were very popular and began to be given twice a week, latterly by Richard Singleton, but were abandoned in 1911 when the **Electric Picture Palace** opened in Stonelaw Road. This long, low structure had a dingy, gas-lit auditorium running parallel to the street with exposed roof trusses and rows of wooden benches on a bare planked floor. Mrs Anna Maxwell went to the Electric as a child in the early twenties:

> The hall was no palace! It was run down and reeked of gas from the lighting. Only silent films were shown in there, with an old woman playing a wee upright piano in the corner. I think the Palace was on its last legs when I knew it.

The Palace never did show talkies. Hopelessly outmoded by 1930, it closed that autumn. The building was used as a billiard hall until 1960.

George Green spread his operations to Rutherglen in 1914, setting up in a solid-looking red brick cinema called the **Pavilion**. Quite close to the Electric Picture Palace, the Pavilion was a cut above it, with plush tip-up seats and a small balcony above the projection box. Eager to keep up with developments, the Greens rebuilt the Pavilion in 1930 and installed talkie apparatus. It was reopened as **Green's Cinema** and showed movies until the autumn of 1959, when it closed, to subsequently become a used car showroom.

In March 1921, the *Rutherglen Reformer* enthused over the opening of the new **Grand Central** cinema on Main Street:

> Shareholders, representatives of the Town Council and local dignitaries graced the proceedings, which began with the National Anthem . . . Afternoon tea was served and a picture programme of comedies and a drama, *Wolves of the Range*, was shown. Mr Powell Edwards, principal baritone of the Beecham Opera, gave effective renderings from his repertoire . . . Internally, the arrangements are all that can be desired, and the visitor will not fail to express admiration and astonishment at the size, comfort and perfect ventilation of the building.

The *Reformer* didn't comment on the fact that the facade was unfinished for the opening. It was two years before enough money was available to complete the large area of cream tiling surrounding a huge advertising hoarding. In the silent era the Grand Central was an outstanding success and it adapted well to the arrival of talkies but in the lean post-war years it was marginalised by the larger super cinemas. Too narrow to be fitted with CinemaScope and plagued by a constantly leaking roof, the Grand Central closed in December 1957 and was demolished.

Two super cinemas arrived in Rutherglen in quick succession. On 23 September 1935, the splendid **Rio** opened for business on Glasgow Road with a novel ceremony, at which Provost John Gilmour read a cable from the filmstar Margaret Sullavan wishing the people of Rutherglen the best of luck with their new cinema, and Sullavan's film *The Good Fairy* was shown to an enthusiastic audience. The impressive Rio, nicknamed the 'R–10' (as was its namesake at Canniesburn Toll), stayed abreast of technical changes. When CinemaScope and stereophonic sound became big attractions, Caledonian Associated Cinemas quickly installed the new systems. But its position on the busy Glasgow Road sealed its fate. It was compulsorily purchased to allow a road improvement to proceed and closed in June 1971 for demolition.

The Rutherglen **Vogue** fared a little better, in that it still exists. Opened hard on the heels of the Rio, on 29 January 1936, it was designed by James McKissack for George Singleton's growing empire. The site was awkward, sloping steeply upwards from Main Street and, despite considerable excavation, it was necessary to build several large

The Grand Central in the late 1930s. (Glasgow Museums)

The Rio in 1969. (Glasgow Museums)

stairways with foyer areas leading up to the auditorium. The waiting rooms, with their Corinthian columns and art deco flourishes, the auditorium, with columns round the proscenium and back-lit embell-ishments on the side walls, and the cove lighting throughout, were unusually opulent for a Singleton cinema.

The Vogue was opened by Harry Lauder and, after George Singleton had praised McKissack for 'a most gracious picture house', the first audience were treated to Cecil B. De Mille's epic *The Crusades*.

In 1936 the Vogue went, with many other Singleton cinemas, to **Odeon**, whose name it was immediately given. The geometric, green, amber and cream tiled facade fitted the new owner's corporate image very well. But even this grand super cinema couldn't survive the sixties slump and closed in October 1974. It became a Top Rank Club and, from 1987, a Mecca bingo hall which, recently renovated, it still is.

The exotic Vogue, here renamed the Odeon, was a landmark on Rutherglen's Main Street. (Glasgow's Museum)

Ibrox, Govan and Paisley Road West

Ibrox

Opened in March 1910 by A.E.Pickard, the **Ibrox Cinematograph Theatre** in Lendel Street was Ibrox's first cinema. Originally the Ibrox and Bellahouston Roller Skating Rink it was converted to plans by Neil C. Duff into a humble, stadium-plan hall with bench seating for about 1,000. It only lasted for about five years and was turned into a factory, the remains of which can still be seen.

The **Lorne**, in Cornwall Street, also designed by Duff, brought the

The Lorne as a bingo hall in the 1970s. (Ian Cunningham)

relative comfort of upholstered, tip-up seats to Ibrox. The Lorne was opened, unfinished, in January 1914, by a local company of which James Galt, the Rangers and Everton football star, was chairman. Nearly the whole Rangers team was at the opening ceremony and Bobby Parker made the trip from Everton to be there. A.B. King was appointed manager of the Lorne and lost no time in booking the latest and best films. Big stars such as Charlie Chaplin and Harold Lloyd were soon drawing great crowds to the new cinema. A year after it opened the *Glasgow Observer* noted:

> The Lorne Cinema House ... falls to be ranked as one of the best of Glasgow's numerous cinema entertainments. The building, which is a handsome and spacious one, is very conveniently situated on the Ibrox (tram) car line and so easy of access from all parts of the city. Having been specially built and not merely adapted for its present purpose, the Lorne Cinema House is a well laid out and comfortable structure. Its appointments and equipment will be found to be quite up to the best city standards. In the films displayed the management is evidently determined to be satisfied with nothing less than the best.

In 1928 Caledon Pictures Ltd became the Lorne's owners and A.B. King became a director. Shortly afterwards, in response to the appearance of a large rival just off Paisley Road West, the building was completely revamped by Gardner and Glen, emerging as a much improved 1,265 seater with a smooth frontage in green and cream faience tiles and a moderne style interior. Ibrox folk remember the Lorne as the friendliest cinema in the district and for its close associations with Rangers. It closed as a cinema in 1968 but lasted another eight years as a bingo hall before it was demolished in 1984.

The Lorne's rival was the mighty **Capitol** in Lorne Street. Had it been run by the Greens (they at one time owned the site and John Fairweather, the architect of their picture houses, designed the building), the Capitol might have become another Playhouse, but its owner was Harry Kemp, a showman with a small circuit of cinemas in the Saltcoats/Stevenston area of Ayrshire. Opened in April 1927 the Capitol represented one of Fairweather's more ingenious schemes. A massive hall on a cramped site up a side street, externally it was unspectacular and, from some angles, ungainly. The side wall stretching along Lorne Street looked more like an engineering works than a place of entertainment. A narrow entrance portico, in English red brick with stone detailing, harmonised neither with the rest of the frontage nor with the rows of tenements surrounding it. The Capitol's

The vast columned auditorium of the Capitol – seen here as a bingo club. (David Trevor Jones)

fascination lay within. As in previous Fairweather projects, the entrance hall was small and oval shaped and almost the entire structure was taken up by the auditorium, along whose side walls brutish Corinthian columns supported neo-classical friezes. The colossal, 1,200 seat circle extended almost to the proscenium and the essential large crush hall occupied a space between the stalls ceiling and the circle steppings. For some a visit to the Capitol must have been frustrating since, from seats near the side walls, only the top third of the screen was visible, but it had other attractions. Edmund Campbell, from Kinning Park, a regular visitor during the thirties, remembers it fondly:

> The Capitol was the grandest of the Ibrox picture houses. It was the only one with a shelter for the audiences to queue in on wet days. While we queued we were well entertained by a variety of turns. There was Dougie the tenor, who stood on a soapbox and sang so loud that he could be heard inside the cinema and the ushers soon came out and chased him away and 'The Darkie', a coloured gentleman who pushed an old pram with a gramophone inside it and played tunes for pennies. My favourite was an acrobat who put a coin on the kerb, did a somersault and picked it up with his tongue.

Big releases often played at the Capitol for several weeks and some of the more popular ones were entertainingly promoted. For the original *Frankenstein*, starring Boris Karloff, life-size models of the monster

90

The Capitol in the 1950s. (Kevin Wheelan)

were displayed in local newsagent's shops. After the Capitol was sold to Gaumont in 1928, when a film packed it out, which was not uncommon, customers who couldn't get in were told which tram would take them to Gaumont's Tivoli in Partick, where the same film would be showing. In 1954 the Capitol took the **Gaumont** name.

When audiences began to decline, the Gaumont's size and poor sight lines were too much of a handicap to continued profitable operation and it was closed in August 1961. Since then the building has had a chequered career as a bingo hall run by Rank, Top Flight, Mecca and now by Rank again. In recent years it has been relatively lightly used and the auditorium is in good condition. Its scale, if nothing else, still impresses.

Govan

Once an independent burgh, now a district of Glasgow, Govan is synonymous with shipbuilding. Famous firms such as Fairfields, Stephens and Harland & Wolff, were the core of the local economy and the ups and downs of the shipyards and their dependent industries affected the entire population. Govan, like the rest of Clydeside, suffered badly in the Great Depression of the 1930s, yet there were always Govanites who had money to spare, even in the not so good times, and many of them were keen cinema goers.

Around the turn of the century travelling showmen set up cinema equipment in venues such as the Pearce Institute and Govan's fine Town Hall, giving performances to an at first merely curious but increasingly enthusiastic public. The earliest record of regular film shows in Govan dates from 1902 when George Urie Scott presented his 'animated pictures' at the **Lyceum** Theatre. The old Lyceum, built in 1899 as a music hall, was a well-known Govan landmark, with a flamboyant, red sandstone corner entrance projecting from the surrounding tenements and rising into a corbelled tower with arcaded

The original Lyceum during 1920s modifications.

windows topped by a giant globe. It originally seated 3,000 in a three-tiered hall with a vertiginous balcony. The Lyceum only became a full-time cinema after a lavish renovation in 1923, when a new foyer, clad in white marble, was built, and the auditorium was restored and redecorated.

A.B. King succeeded Scott in the management of the Lyceum, which became the first cinema in the district to show talkies when he booked Alfred Hitchcock's thriller *Blackmail*. The early musical *Showboat*, starring Laura La Plante, was particularly memorable as the first half was silent while the second was an 'all talking extravaganza'. Such spectaculars ensured the Lyceum's reputation as the biggest and best cinema in the Govan of the twenties. King's showmanship was imaginative and the staff often dressed up for special occasions. When the Eddie Cantor film, *The Man from Mexico*, was showing the ushers and usherettes delighted the audience by appearing in Mexican costume, complete with ponchos and sombreros.

The Lyceum was totally refurbished in 1932. Charles J. McNair designed the new interior, with a single large balcony, seating extending beyond where the old stage had been and a new proscenium beyond that. Sadly this phase of the Lyceum's career was to be brief; the building was totally destroyed by fire on the night of 23 October 1937.

Govan's first full-time cinema was the **Govan Cross Picture Palace**, opened in 1910. James Hamilton, a local entrepreneur, took over the short-lived Govan Cross Roller Skating Rink, a converted industrial building at the junction of Helen Street and Robert Street, and converted it again, this time into a simple hall with bench seating. Despite the persistent industrial overtones, the Picture Palace was fairly popular but, by the late twenties, the second part of its advertising slogan 'Govan's First and Still the Best' was clearly no longer accurate. It reverted to use as a workshop in 1929.

In February 1912, George Green opened his second *Picturedrome*, in another abandoned roller skating rink, in Summerstoun Road. The adverts read:

GREEN'S GOVAN PICTUREDROME OPENS TOMORROW

COMPLETE PICTURE PROGRAMME
THE PICK OF THE WORLD'S PRODUCTIONS
People's Prices – Pit 2d – Stalls 4d – Balcony (plush tip-ups) 6d
In Order To Place This Entertainment Within The Reach Of All
There Will Be A Few Seats At One Penny
Twice Nightly 7 and 9

The *Govan Press* greeted the new cinema with enthusiasm:

On the opening night at both performances there were a number of films characteristic of Mr Green for excellence and steadiness. A capital variety turn was introduced during the course of the evening, of which the audience was thoroughly appreciative. For the following week Mr Green has personally selected a star series of pictures which will include a representation of the Irish drama *Arrah-Na-Pogue*.

The children's matinee shows were said to be 'of an exceptionally educational character, including travel pictures, which are the best known means of inculcating into the young mind an idea of what geography really is'. But the Picturedrome wasn't perfect. It was in the middle of a large development which also housed a boxing arena and the shouts of the boxing spectators could often be heard in the cinema. Far from being inculcated with an 'idea of what geography really is', the children who trooped along to the 10 o'clock 'penny crush' frequently ignored the films and played Cowboys and Indians in the warren of passages.

In 1931 the Greens leased the Picturedrome to its manager, John Lawrence. It became the Grange Music Hall, but it survived only until 1933 when it was demolished.

The simply named **Govan Cinema**, opened in June 1913, was the district's first purpose-built picture house. One of the earliest cinemas of which John Maxwell was a director, it had an exuberant red sandstone frontage with overtones of the Indian Raj in its curved arches and domed towers. The entrance hall, cleverly arranged with payboxes on either side, led to the better upholstered seats in the middle and rear stalls while a door at the other end of the building served the 2d section with its red leather covered benches. The auditorium was lofty and attractively decorated with plaster swags and garlands, though its basic construction was evident from the exposed iron roof trusses. A Mr Milne, former curator of Pollokshaws Burgh Halls, was appointed manager and declared that the Govan Cinema would aim to attract a 'better class of patron' by screening 'the latest and best pictures of the highest standard'. The opening feature was Abel Gance's epic *Napoleon*, which proved immensely popular. The Govan Cinema's initial popularity continued to such an extent that it could not cope with demand and, in 1934, was demolished to make way for ABC to build a brand new super cinema on the site (see below).

By contrast with Mr Milne's aspirations, A.B. King declared his **Elder** cinema in Reid Street 'the picture house for the masses and not the classes'. Opened in December 1916, the Elder took its unusual name from the fact that the Fairfield shipyard across the road was founded in 1864 by John Elder, who is credited with the invention of the compound steam engine, and whose many industrial endeavours brought prosperity and acclaim to Govan.

The Elder was designed by Albert Gardner and, like most of his cinema designs, was stylistically haphazard. The angular frontage had some unusual elements, not least an advertising tower at one corner, a forerunner of a common feature in cinema design twenty years later. The entrance hall, with its pilasters and ornate plasterwork, was said to have 'a quiet Venetian aspect', and the auditorium was decorated with flower and landscape murals. The pink-corduroy upholstered seats were a first for Govan and an unusual touch in any contemporary suburban cinema.

The Elder started its career inauspiciously when the directors were fined £100 for overlooking the wartime requirement for cinema builders to apply to the Ministry of Munitions for a building licence, but it was soon going from strength to strength. Govan audiences were gluttons for suspense and in the twenties and thirties King booked many classic gangster movies for the Elder. Queues stretched right round the block for the continuous performances of James Cagney and Edward G. Robinson films. As people waited patiently, often in the rain, they were entertained by buskers like the man who would tap-dance on a wooden board and invite them to sing 'Yellow Tram to Bellahouston'. Then the fearsome doorman, dressed in his tightly belted overcoat with red epaulettes would emerge. As the crowd surged forward, he'd bellow, 'Stoap!', and, brandishing his index finger, 'there's only room for wan!'

The Elder was in time marginalised by newer and better appointed neighbours and became an early victim of the spread of television. It closed as a cinema in March 1959 to become a bingo hall called the New Vogue, but was not successful. It closed and lay derelict until it was demolished in 1977.

The only cinema to appear in Govan in the twenties was the **Lyric**, which opened in October 1922 in a back court entered through a shop unit in Langlands Road. Designed by McNair and owned by the Langlands Picture House Ltd, it showed films until March 1933 when it was converted and run as a ballroom until its closure in 1937.

McNair's next Govan project was more auspicious. The **Plaza** was an imposing super opened by ABC in December 1936 on the site of the old Govan Cinema. Its elegant curving frontage swept back to

The Plaza when new in 1937. (Strathclyde Regional Archives)

bulky rear quarters with seating for over two thousand and both the circle and the stalls were divided into front and rear sections with separate entrances (a feature of most early Scottish ABC cinemas which was only abandoned when it was found to waste more money on extra staff than it gained by keeping queues in order). In the midthirties, Govanites' imaginations were captured by the launching of the *Empress of Britain* and the *Empress of Japan*, luxury liners built by Fairfields for Canadian Pacific, and the style of their highly acclaimed interiors was echoed in the Plaza with its cove lighting and combination of glossy veneers with autumnal tints of beige and orange. The passageways were thickly carpeted in red, orange and black and the screen curtains were a gorgeous red with silver appliqué stars. A series of backlit, silvered coves framed the proscenium.

The Plaza was renamed **ABC** in 1966 and closed down in April 1972 with a programme which, appropriately, included *The Last Run*. Glasgow Corporation demolished the building to facilitate road straightening at Govan Cross.

A.B. King commissioned McNair to design a new **Lyceum** around the time the pavilions for the 1938 Empire Exhibition were under construction in nearby Bellahouston Park. The design undoubtedly benefitted from the architectural high which that *tour de force* of

96

streamlined art deco created. The new building was distinguished by a three storey high, curtain-wall frontage which swept round the corner of Govan Road and McKechnie Street in a graceful curve. Above the doorway, five tall, recessed windows of beautifully backlit, green glass blocks were separated by soaring blue-tiled mullions. The rest of the exterior was finished in tiles and brickwork with the flowing lines emphasised by a black cornice.

The 1938 Lyceum – easily Glasgow's most spectacular suburban cinema design. (Strathclyde Regional Archives)

The foyer was decorated with palm motifs and had an terrazzo floor with curving streamlined patterns radiating from a circular island pay-box (where 'wee Ina', the cashier, always had a friendly word for regular customers). Softly lit portraits of the great movie stars smiled down from the walls on the queues below. In the oval lounge the lofty curving walls were decorated with a mural of famous Govan-built liners, naïve paintings of shipyard life, Walt Disney characters and even the Loch Ness Monster, all in streamline moderne style. Flowing lines dominated the auditorium too; elegant wood-veneer dados swept towards the decorative grilles on either side of the screen and concealed lighting curled across the ceiling suffusing everything in blue, pink and lilac. It was a perfect venue for the MGM musical spectaculars of the day, resembling the set of one.

With 2,600 seats the Lyceum was Govan's largest cinema, exuding grandeur and opulence. Gracie Fields and Victor McLagen in *We're Going To Be Rich* was completely in keeping for the opening in December 1938. So was the Lyceum's licensee and manager Ian

Bryson J.P., a local celebrity who came to be known as 'Mr Govan'. Bryson sported a waxed moustache and always appeared in full evening dress to bid his customers goodnight. His charming personality and hard work and A.B. King's booking skills made the Lyceum a classy cinema throughout its long career.

Despite its great size, the Lyceum lasted the longest of all the Govan cinemas, only closing temporarily when it was sold to the Paulo family in 1974 for bingo. The Govanites did not relinquish their favourite picture house without a struggle and a timely petition was initiated by a local minister to persuade the authorities only to grant the bingo licence if a cinema facility was retained. 'What will the children do on Saturday afternoons without their matinee?' he argued. As a result, when the Lyceum re-opened later that year, part of the circle had been screened off as a 480 seat cinema. It was Glasgow's first and only cine-bingo operation.

The Paulos were no novices at film exhibition. In the thirties Sam Paulo had taken travelling cinema shows round the miners' welfare halls of Lanarkshire and Ayrshire and another branch of the family had shares in three fine super cinemas close to Edinburgh (all called County, the name chosen for the Lyceum's bingo operation). At a time when many cinemagoers were responding to the often lurid X-rated programmes by staying at home and many cinemas were losing support through being unable to secure quality films on a regular basis, the Lyceum management solved the problem by reviving the Fred Astaire and Ginger Rogers musicals which had made it famous in the first place. People came to Govan from all over the city to wallow in nostalgia.

In the mid-seventies the Lyceum found itself in the media spotlight when it was hired for trade union meetings during the months of strife at Upper Clyde Shipbuilders which affected so many Govan workers. Unfortunately, around the same time it also became a hangout for vandals and drug users and, when Ian Bryson retired, it was doomed as a picture house. No more films were shown after January 1981, since when it has been a bingo hall.

On 4 July 1938, George Singleton added 2,500 cinema seats to Govan's already impressive total when he opened his latest **Vogue** in Langlands Road with *Varsity Show*, starring Dick Powell and Ted Healey. The Govan Vogue was its owner's favourite suburban cinema:

Our architect, James McKissack, really did us proud at Govan. The Vogue had more neon lighting than any other cinema in the suburbs. It cost so much in electricity that it was switched off as

The gleaming tiled Vogue in 1938. (Scottish Film Archive)

soon as everybody was inside and stayed off until the films were over. I flew up from London in 1939 and, approaching the old airfield at Renfrew, I was so proud to see my cinema glowing down below. It really was quite an attraction. I don't know why we painted the interior in cream, orange, green and gold. Painting a cinema in the colours of the Irish tricolour was not a good idea in staunchly loyalist Govan.

Perhaps seeing tramcars in the same colour scheme every day pacified the Orangemen for the Vogue was a very busy cinema.

The magnificent gently curved frontage was subtly clad in cream and buff faience tiles. Inside, the decor was elegantly simple, highlighting the proscenium arch with its heavy ogee curve and framing panels of bas-relief plasterwork in stripes and stylised leaf shapes. The streamline architraves around the doors were a McKissack hallmark.

In December 1961 the Singletons leased the Vogue for bingo sessions. When they realised how potentially lucrative this could be they displaced the tenants and Vogue bingo continued under Singleton control until 1985, when a generous offer from a property developer was accepted. The building was demolished and an infill block of flats was erected on the site.

In its pre-war heyday, Govan could boast some 8,500 cinema seats. Sixty years on, there is no cinema in Govan, the Lyceum alone survives as a place of entertainment and the former Fairfield works is Govan's last shipyard.

Paisley Road West

Paisley Road West is a long arterial route linking central Glasgow to the burgh of Paisley. The *Scenic Picture House* at Paisley Round Toll brought cinema to the area in 1912. It was an 800 seat, nickelodeon-type in a back court, entered down a flight of steps below the tenements and, according to Mrs Jean Melvin, was a pretty disgusting place:

> We got in with two jam jars. It was a dark, dank hall with wooden forms to sit on and a gently sloping wooden floor – and it stank! Us kids loved the old Chaplin, Harold Lloyd and Pearl White films that they showed us there and some weans wouldn't even miss a minute or two to go to the toilet; so their mothers said, 'jist dae it oan the flair'. The Scenic fairly ran with pee at the end of these matinee shows.

The Scenic was joined in 1921 by the **Imperial** across the road. Run by Henry Meiklejohn, who had the Grand Central in Jamaica Street, it was a conversion from old stables to plans by William Beresford Inglis. The transformation was so ingenious that it would have been almost impossible to guess its origins. The Scenic was closed in 1938. The larger, grander Imperial outlasted it by over twenty years, but by the end of the Second World War, it had gone far downhill. After a fire in 1952, it was rebuilt with a striking moderne interior overlaid with 'Festival of Britain' touches, but it only continued as a cinema until 1959. The structure still exists as the 'Grand Ole Opry', a unique social club for Glasgow's many Country and Western fans. With shooting galleries, bars and a dance floor the one-time Imperial is a popular meeting place for cowboys and cowgirls from all over the city and further afield.

Further west was the **Mosspark Picture House**, a much-loved little cinema built in 1925 and known to local folk as the 'Mossie'. Designed by its builder, it looked more like a village hall than a cinema

Ibrox, Govan and Paisley Road West

The proscenium of the Imperial after rebuilding in 1952.

The Mosspark Picture House. (Strathclyde Regional Archives)

'Cunard' and 'Standard' tramcars pass the Westway in the 1950s. (J.J.W. Richards)

and the film shows were organised by the proprietor/manager. In 1938 the 'Mossie' was sold to the Caledonian Associated Cinemas subsidiary, Scottish Central Cinemas, and continued to serve its clientele quietly until November 1973, when it closed with Marlon Brando in *Last Tango in Paris*. By that time CAC had diversified into property speculation and no doubt saw the 'Mossie' site as potentially profitable. The cinema was replaced by a block of flats.

George Smith and James Welsh added the **Westway** to Paisley Road West's cinemas in 1935. Designed by Bryden, Robertson and Boyd it had an austere facade in which three tall, mullioned windows above the canopy led the eye upwards to the cinema's name in large stone letters set in a recess. The auditorium was at right angles to the entrance with a single storey office-cum-waiting-area in between. The plain interior had a horseshoe-shaped balcony.

The Singleton circuit bought the Westway in January 1950 but, doubtless realising that the area had too many cinemas, they closed it in 1959 and converted it into a dance hall called the Flamingo. Local folk, perhaps unaware of the Las Vegas gambling palace after which

102

The mighty Aldwych when new in 1939. (Strathclyde Regional Archives)

it was named, persisted in referring to it as the 'Flaming-O'. When ballroom dancing also declined in popularity, bingo was introduced and nowadays the old Westway prospers as a Mecca club. Although all evidence of its original use is gone it is, ironically since it was the first to close, the only surviving cinema building in the area.

Cardonald's biggest and grandest cinema, the magnificent **Aldwych**, was opened in April 1938, a logical progression for George Smith and James Welsh's Westway Cinema Ltd. The first performances featured the pre-war technicolour epic *The Adventures of Robin Hood*, starring Errol Flynn and Olivia de Havilland. James McKissack's largest cinema design and one of the most lavish suburban picture houses in Scotland, the Aldwych was something of an epic in its own right. The imposing, ultra modern looking exterior was smoothly rendered with horizontal stripes of cream and amber tiles alternating up to the door tops. A hefty cornice carried all round the top of the building unified the design. The interior was restrained yet conceived on a grand scale. The side walls tapered gently towards the proscenium and parallel neon strips flowed towards the curtains whose pattern echoed the striped wall decoration.

As an example of cinema architecture, the Aldwych was one of Glasgow's finest, even if some found its severe lines too plain and its squarish mass too heavy. As a business, however, it ultimately proved a grand folly; a cinema superfluous to Cardonald's needs. The Aldwych, along with the Westway, joined the Singleton circuit in 1950 giving George Singleton a 3,800 seat virtual monopoly in the Cardonald area, and, renamed the **Vogue**, it came through the fifties quite well. But by 1963 business was poor and the decision was taken to close it. It was leased for bingo but this lasted only a few months and by 1964 it was empty again. It was sold to Safeway who opened a supermarket on the site. The last of Singleton's Vogues to open, it became one of the first to close.

The influence of the Empire Exhibition on mainstream cinema architecture in Scotland has been noted in connection with the Govan Lyceum, but it had generally been overlooked that an exotic little picture house was actually part of the Exhibition. Although the *Empire Cinema* had a very futuristic appearance, it was surely the shortest lived purpose built cinema building in the city. The Exhibition was held in Bellahouston Park from 3 May to 29 October 1938 and Alister G. MacDonald, famous for his many streamlined news theatres in and around London and for his attractive reconstruction of La Scala in Sauchiehall Street, designed both the Empire Cinema and the Peace Pavilion. The exterior of the 600 seat cinema was dominated by three soaring fins above the entrance and the foyer was semicircular with glass walls. It was used mostly for showing hour-long newsreels but it also had a stage for live performances. After the Exhibition closed both MacDonald's innovative buildings were dismantled (the Peace Pavilion must have seemed startlingly incongruous in a Britain by then at war with Nazi Germany).

The West End

Anderston/Finnieston

For tidiness' sake, the 'West End' has been taken here to mean the area west of Charing Cross and Anderston Cross and between the River Clyde and Great Western Road. It therefore includes not only the wealthy districts usually referred to as 'the West End' but the less well off districts along the north bank of the river, starting, on the edge of the city centre, with Anderston and Finnieston.

The **Gaiety Theatre** at Anderston Cross had been a variety theatre under various names for over ten years when, in the autumn of 1909, J.J. Bennell began to present his cinema shows there. The programmes were shared with his Wellington Palace in the Gorbals and a 'runner' was given the tram fare to carry the spools between the two venues. Variety acts supplemented the film shows until the fifties, Anderston folk enjoyed a sing-along just as much as the movies, but the standards of showmanship were sometimes pretty poor. A friend of the author remembers that:

> One night one of the variety turns was a strong man who lifted various heavy-looking objects. At the end of his act he challenged anybody in the audience to lift a particularly large weight for a three shilling reward. My brother was just a wee fellow but he needed the money. He went up on stage and proceeded to lift the iron bar, without much effort and to great applause! When we went to collect his prize money after the show we were chased out of the building by the manager and my brother never got a penny of his reward.

The Gaiety had several strong-arm men, who were not averse to roughing up and throwing out anyone who made trouble, like the lad who persisted in dropping lighted matches from the balcony into the stalls.

George Urie Scott was running the Gaiety when, in 1935, its interior was remodelled from a three to a two tiered configuration, but this was due to a shortage of fire exits in its upper balcony rather than to any aspiration to grandeur, and the rudimentary old picture house had to wait some time for its moment of glory. That moment came when a smouldering cigarette end, left after a boxing match, started a fire which devastated the nearby St Andrews Halls, Glasgow's magnificent concert venue, whose splendid auditorium, with its exceptional acoustics, hosted world-class performers. A new concert venue was urgently needed and Glasgow Corporation commandeered the Gaiety, giving it a very necessary facelift. It opened as the Glasgow Concert Hall in January 1963 with a performance of children's classics by the Scottish National Orchestra, whose temporary home it became. Many internationally renowned singers and orchestras performed in this shabby old cinema but the inappropriateness of the arrangement seemed to epitomise the cultural and architectural decline of the city at the time. Almost inevitably, the Gaiety's great days were few. The City Halls in Candleriggs were renovated as Glasgow's main concert hall and the doors of the old Gaiety closed for the last time on 31 July 1968. It was pulled down shortly afterwards to enable the Anderston redevelopment to be completed.

The **West End Electric Theatre** had a very short life. Opened in 1910 on the south side of Sauchiehall Street, just west of Charing Cross, it had a very peculiar accommodation arrangement. Two auditoria shared one screen at the apex of an L-shaped interior. In such a relatively quiet residential part of the street and with such an impractical design it is hardly surprising that this most awkward of cinemas survived for only three years.

The union, in 1900, of the United Presbyterians with part of the Free Church to form the United Free Church created a superfluity of church buildings. Two of these became Anderston cinemas.

The **Grove** in Breadalbane Street was a conversion to plans by Albert Gardner of the Sandyford United Free Church, and was opened in 1915. Part of the notorious James Graham circuit, in the late twenties and early thirties this spartan cinema was often the subject of press reports about attacks on staff, as though it had become a hangout for thugs, and it closed in January 1932. The Kent Road West United Free Church became the unremarkable **New Kent** cinema in 1921 and operated until May 1931. The Grove and the New Kent, like so many other smaller picture houses, good and bad, foundered in the face of competition from the new generation of super cinemas.

The **Kelvin**, which opened in May 1930 at 1073 Argyle Street was the district's first and only super cinema. The last collaboration between the architects A.V. Gardner and W.R. Glen, the Kelvin was a bizarre mixture of geometric forms and multiple roof levels with an

octagonal stair tower at one corner. The auditorium in this extraordinary edifice was clad, roof and walls, in asbestos panels. *Bioscope* magazine's description of its 'admirable – and thoroughly Scottish – combination of the practical and the artistic' was incredible considering that the Kelvin's interior was devised in a semi-atmospheric manner with a Turkish mosque on one side of the screen and a Spanish scene on the other and that the hall had a horseshoe-shaped balcony and side waiting areas, which were very antiquated after the advent of talkies.

The Kelvin initially belonged to Kelvin Cinema Ltd of which John Maxwell was a director, and Maxwell's ABC booked its films for the first two years. After failing to acquire outright control of the Kelvin, Maxwell withdrew from its board and the majority of the shares went to George Taylor who ran a circuit of poor quality picture houses catering to the lower end of the market. During his management the Kelvin went downhill, especially after the war when rationing of materials hampered maintenance work. The Kelvin closed in 1959 and has changed hands several times since. As the Kelvin Sports Arena it hosted boxing and wrestling matches which, in the sixties, were often televised. Mecca then tried to run it as a bingo club and, when that failed, it became a night club. After a spell of dereliction it is now the Crème de la Crème, which claims to be the world's largest Indian restaurant. The frontage has been restored to suit its present use but

*The 'atmospheric'
auditorium of the
Kelvin when new.*

107

none of the atmospheric interior decoration remains.

Partick

Starting in 1909, films were shown three times a week in the ramshackle former Alexandra Hall, hidden in a back court at 95 Dumbarton Road, and about a decade later the venue became a full-time cinema, known as the **Standard.** It was owned by James Graham, and its nickname, the 'Palais de Scratch' (a reference to Fyfe & Fyfe's luxurious Palais de Danse in the next block, which was also sometimes used as a cinema) indicates its quality. Duncan Cree remembers matinee performances at the Standard in the early thirties:

> We were jammed onto long wooden benches at the front of the hall. There was loud cheering when the lights dimmed for a singsong led by the lady pianist. The words were projected onto the screen:
>
> > 'Don't throw stones at your mother,
> > She'll wash you and put you to bed.
> > Don't throw stones at your mother,
> > Throw bricks at your father instead!'

The uproarious and verminous Standard, along with James Graham's other disreputable picture houses, passed, in 1945 to A.B. King's Glasgow and West of Scotland Cinemas and, despite deterioration due to wartime building materials control, it stayed in business until its licence was revoked in 1957.

A couple of blocks along Dumbarton Road, the purpose built **Garrick** opened in January 1916. Being almost at the gates of the Western Infirmary it was soon renamed the **Western**. Initially a narrow fronted building with an outsize sunburst over the entrance and curious scrolls in vaguely Spanish style at roof level, it was doubled in size and the auditorium turned to run parallel to the street when the adjacent buildings were demolished in 1921. By the sixties the Western had become almost as squalid as the Standard had been and it closed in 1966 to lie derelict until its demolition in 1978.

The **Partick Picture House**, opened in Vine Street, also in 1916, was even stranger looking than the Western. A bizarre and banal design by A.V. Gardner, its eccentric medieval-style exterior had two function-less turrets, Greek masks on either side of the doorway and a unicorn's head protruding from the facade. The inside, which featured

The Western Cinema c. 1920. (Strathclyde Regional Archives)

109

Gardner's favoured horseshoe treatment of the balcony, was more conventional. The Partick's chequered history included being destroyed by fire in 1929 and rebuilt and extended to open in 1931 as the 1,800 seat **New Partick**. John Maxwell had an interest in the company which originally opened the Partick and around this time ABC was booking films for both it and the Kelvin. Both were sold to George Taylor in 1931 when Maxwell withdrew his interest to concentrate on the nationwide expansion of ABC. A second disastrous fire, ironically during a week when *The Burning Hills* was the main feature, forced the New Partick to shut permanently in 1962. The building was repaired and served as a warehouse for many years before it was knocked down.

A.B. King's **Rosevale** at 467 Dumbarton Road was pitched at a superior sector of the market. The biggest Glasgow cinema to be built into a tenement back court, it is the only surviving example of this once common type. Built in 1921, the cavernous, 1,894 seat auditorium was entered via a long corridor through the ground floor of a tenement. It had a simple barrel-vaulted ceiling with decorative niches and columns on the side walls. When new it reverberated to the sound of a Christie organ, whose pipes were concealed behind ornate grilles on either side of the plain proscenium, but the instrument was removed in 1937 and, according to devotees, the Rosevale was never the same.

Picture houses in back courts not only robbed the occupants of the surrounding tenements of their drying and playing areas but also blocked out daylight and prevented fresh air from entering their homes. Nevertheless, in the twenties, Glasgow Corporation usually granted permission for their construction. Cinemas offered cheap, local entertainment for poorer citizens and provided a warm sheltered place away from the cramped conditions of many homes. It kept some out of the pubs and others out of trouble. These considerations were felt to outweigh any possible nuisance factors.

In March 1932, the Rosevale was rather unorthodoxly enlarged and thoroughly modernised. With business as usual, buildings behind it were demolished and an extension to the auditorium built. Then the cinema had only to be closed for a few days while the wall between the old and new sections was taken down and the whole interior handsomely redecorated, with murals of Highland scenes in the crush halls and a striking, cove-lit, silver curtained proscenium and modern light fittings, hanging from the elegant, curved ceiling, in the new

2,000 seat auditorium. Although privately operated, the Rosevale managed to stay in business until 1965, after which it housed bingo sessions until 1982, when it was converted into a snooker club. A decade later it became a discount supermarket.

Hillhead and Partickhill

Dumbarton Road was a social dividing line; coalmen were known to raise their prices when crossing from south to north. To the south were docklands, shipyards and working class housing. To the north was Partickhill, with its cricket ground, from which villas and fine sandstone tenements with 'wally' (tiled) closes and spacious rooms stretched through Hyndland, Dowanhill and Hillhead to Great Western Road. In the days when coal was king and air pollution from smoking chimneys sometimes blanketed large areas of the city, the prevailing westerly winds ensured a healthier atmosphere on this high ground to the west and here some of Glasgow's wealthiest suburbs grew up.

Some of the these West End suburbs never allowed a cinema or any place of popular entertainment to gain a foothold; the residents were well-enough off to travel into the city centre for their entertainment and would not tolerate having their respectability disturbed by gaudy cinema buildings or unsightly crowds. The former burgh of Hillhead (it was absorbed into the city of Glasgow in 1891) was a little different. It began to develop into Glasgow's 'Latin Quarter' after the University moved there in 1870, and its inhabitants were some of the city's staunchest filmgoers. Partickhill folk were also fond of a good film and supported one of the city's more unusual suburban cinemas.

The **Hillhead Picture Salon** was opened in 1913 and proved an enduring success. The long, low building was typical of purpose built picture houses of the period, but the quality of the detailing and the use of structural ferroconcrete frames made it exceptional. At a time when highly flammable nitrate spools were a great fire risk and fires often caused ceiling collapses in buckling iron and steel structures, concrete proved a safer option for cinema construction. The Salon's elegant frontage was crowned with a dome under which the cast iron entrance canopy was topped with stucco garlands. Five tall, Glasgow-style art nouveau frieze panels adorned the main wall, and even minor fixtures such as rone pipes were ornamented with cast iron lion's head masks.

In pre-First World War days patrons were greeted by the com-

The Salon nears closure in the summer of 1992. (Author)

manding figure of the doorman, with a waxed moustache and in a military-style brown uniform with gold braid. Having bought tickets they would be ushered through mauve drapes, adding to the allure and mystery of the experience, into the Salon's beautiful little auditorium with its deeply coffered ceiling, moulded plaster garlands decorating the walls and small balcony at the rear above the projection box. The music of the Salon's orchestra, led by Herr Wilhelm Iff, a portly gentleman who had previously worked in the famous Empire Theatre in the city centre, created an atmosphere to suit the show, but during the First World War the Salon reverberated to the sound of an American jazz band whose black singer caused a sensation with such songs as 'My Curly Headed Baby'. While the band played, tea and biscuits were served from silver trays.

Unfortunately, by the fifties the Salon had gone into what looked like a terminal decline. The strictures of post-war life and the imposition of Entertainment Tax at the flat rate of 2¼d on a 5d ticket (almost 47%) prevented exhibitors from investing in their properties. But despite worn out seats and grubby carpets it survived thanks to the good relationship between management and customers. Film enthusiast, Ian Miller of Bearsden, recalls that the staff were always eager to please: 'One could always request a film from the management. If you could persuade five or six friends to ask for *Whisky Galore* to be shown, it would be sure to turn up a couple of weeks later and play to good attendances for several nights'. This was possible because the

Brook family who owned the Salon at that time had once represented 20th Century Fox in Glasgow and had many contacts in the film rental business. University staff, students and other West End devotees were loyal patrons.

In 1969 the Partick-based entertainment company Fyfe & Fyfe Ltd bought the Salon and renovated it in opulent style. New seats and carpets were fitted and the fabric of the building was repaired. The original, and by then leaking, dome was replaced and the foyer redesigned. The Salon was confidently re-opened with *The Sound of Music* in April 1970 and these very necessary alterations ensured it another two decades of life. But although the refurbishment did wonders for business, Fyfe & Fyfe found it increasingly difficult to secure suitable films for their only picture house and it came under threat once again. Rumours circulated that it might become an Angus Steak House or a disco and the neighbouring Western Baths Club eyed it jealously with a view to setting up squash courts. In 1987, Caledonian Associated Cinemas, who owned the twin-screen Grosvenor further along Byres Road, bought the Salon, gaining a cinema monopoly in Hillhead.

CAC introduced plush new red seats, a new screen with silver curtains and a harmonious pale blue and cream colour scheme and the Salon emerged, in 1988, as the best cinema auditorium in the city at that time (and the only one with a balcony which still had double seats for courting couples). With access to both the Odeon and Cannon film releases each week, CAC could put the movie with the widest appeal into the larger Salon and show the lesser attraction at the Grosvenor. With an upturn in cinema attendances forecast, hopes were high that the Salon would have a bright and secure future but, regrettably, not enough people could be wooed in to enjoy the good films in an atmosphere of *fin de siècle* splendour and CAC had to close it.

The manner of the closure caused CAC to be pilloried in the press coverage which followed. On 12 October 1992, during a successful run of Disney's *Beauty and the Beast*, staff came to work as usual to find that they had been locked out. Workmen had begun removing the seats for storage and, when the manageress tried to prevent this, the police were called to eject her from the building. It was a tense, yet farcical spectacle. Local feeling ran high and 'Save Our Salon', a lobbying group supported by such celebrities as Sean Connery, David Puttnam and Sir Richard Attenborough, was formed. A 15,000 signature petition was collected calling for the cinema to be re-opened. Meanwhile, CAC tried to sell the building to the Western Baths Club next door, but a planning enquiry rejected the Club's proposals and

The Grosvenor in November 1951. (Allen Eyles Collection)

sentiment hardened against CAC. The Salon had to be a proper cinema or nothing. Even an imaginative scheme from CAC's parent company, Haymarket Leisure, to restore the building as 'Salon – Cinema City', a 'Planet Hollywood type, multi-media dining experience' combining a cinema and a restaurant, was opposed. At present the Salon's doors remain closed. CAC are unlikely to sell it to any rival to the Grosvenor and the longer the building is unused the less likely it is to become a picture house again.

The **Grosvenor**, first opened in May 1921, was built to a remarkably forward-looking design by Gardner and Glen. Behind the narrow but striking tiled entrance on Byres Road, were a simple auditorium which tapered towards the screen and, above the foyer, a cafe and American-style soda fountain. It was described in the press as 'the most up-to-date picture theatre in Glasgow . . . renowned for excellent pictures combined with delightful musical accompaniments'. In the autumn of 1929 the Grosvenor was bought by John Maxwell's ABC circuit. It was so popular that the cafe was abandoned to create extra waiting rooms. Boxes at the rear of the stalls could be hired by groups of five for 2/6d (14p), a great attraction for students. On Saturday mornings there was a children's club, the ABC Minors, and the rest of the week continuous performances were given from midday onwards. After over fifty years of constant, punishing use the Grosvenor was beginning to look dilapidated when, in May 1976, ABC sold the by

114

The Tivoli in 1945.
(Kevin Wheelan)

now only marginally profitable operation to CAC. It was run on a 'care and maintenance' basis for the next four years before being given a radical remodelling. The original entrance on Byres Road was sealed up and later replaced by a restaurant. Two new, small, luxury cinemas, the Ashton and the Kelvin, were created in the former stalls area, entered from Ashton Lane, where trendy bars and eating places now flank the cinemas. The new complex opened in December 1980 with *The Deerhunter* and *Heartbeat* in the Kelvin and Edward Woodward in *Breaker Morant* in the Ashton. CAC recently proposed additional screens in the old circle area and the Grosvenor's busy location looks likely to ensure its continued success.

The **Tivoli**, on the Partickhill stretch of Crow Road, was a classy cinema. Designed by William J. Blain of Denny & Blain, a Dumbarton-based firm, it had a severe exterior, finished in red sandstone and facing brick, whose epic, neo-classical styling was most evident in the entrance portico, which protruded from the frontage and served as a waiting hall. The pilastered walls and black-and-white-tile terrazzo floor suggested a Roman villa. Everything about the Tivoli was conceived on a grand scale; wide staircases carried customers up to the pay-boxes and grand inner foyer, the 1,900 seat auditorium was the size of an aircraft hanger and slips from the vast balcony extended almost to the proscenium. The rows were so wide that customers could come and go without seated visitors having to move. Although the Roman-style decoration seemed sparse, it was of good quality. A Christie organ was fitted to woo people from the Rosevale, where the music was a big crowd puller.

The Tivoli was opened by Councillor Thomas Kelly on 29 April 1929, showing *Wings*, starring Clara Rew and Charles Rodgers. In 1932, its owner, Thomas Ormiston Ltd, was absorbed by the ever-expanding Gaumont British group giving the Tivoli access to the most recent Gaumont films with their wide audience appeal. Compared to the peerless Ascot (see below), Gaumont's other West End cinema, the Tivoli seemed rather old-fashioned and too lofty. It had a name for being dimly lit and, by the fifties, smoke-stained, but it was cheaper, generally showed newer films and attracted livelier audiences. When *Rock Around The Clock*, with Bill Haley and the Comets, was shown in October 1959, the audience got up and danced in the aisles.

After the Second World War, Gaumont came under Rank control and, in December 1967, the Tivoli became one of many of their marginally profitable picture houses sold to Classic Cinemas, which already ran three Glasgow city centre cinemas and was rapidly expanding throughout Britain. The building was given a cursory over-haul and the name changed to the **Classic**. It soldiered on, presenting a wide variety of films, often in repertory, with as many as six different programmes a week. Classic Cinemas itself became the subject of a successful takeover bid by the Laurie Marsh group, which went heavily into debt as a result of the purchase and tried to cut its losses by selling a number of cinemas. The Classic was a casualty and closed on 26 February 1972. At the time it was showing *The Prime of Miss Jean Brodie, Butch Cassidy and the Sundance Kid, Desert Tanks, The Unholy Four* and *New Face in Hell*, a diverse selection typical of the Classic's eclectic booking policy. The newspaper announcement read, 'Power Cut – Cinema Temporarily Closed', but when the Classic re-opened soon afterwards it was a County bingo hall.

Whiteinch and Scotstoun

The **Paladium** cinema, the one-time Whiteinch Roller Skating Rink, was packing in the crowds from 1910 until it was closed and demol-ished in 1924 and the Avenue, further along Dumbarton Road, began doing brisk business as soon as it opened it 1913. Originally built as a music hall, the **Avenue** represented the sort of mixed architecture so despised by critics of early cinema design. Designed by Thomas Baird Jnr, architect of the Moorish Salon in Sauchiehall Street, the Avenue's

florid frontage in French Empire style was tacked onto the plain brick body of the building. The facade had towers with pyramidal roofs flanking a high arch and was elaborately decorated with scrollwork and swags. In contrast, the interior was austere, with only the simplest plaster scrollwork on the balcony front. The Avenue joined James Graham's circuit in 1919 and, in 1930, was renovated to plans by Lennox and McMath and renamed the **Victoria**. In 1945 it was sold to George Palmer's Associated GP Cinemas, but its condition by then seems to have persuaded its new owner to distance himself from it. Rather than being renamed the George in common with his other cinemas, the Victoria became the **Victory** to mark the end of the Second World War. Refurbished, it soldiered on until 1964, when it became a warehouse. It was demolished in 1980.

The Victory as a warehouse in the 1960s. (The late Frank Worsdall)

Still further west along Dumbarton Road, the **Premier**, opened in 1922, was a simple conversion from the Victoria Billiard Hall, with rows of benches on a flat wooden floor. The advent of talkies closed this little known venue in 1930.

The Singletons pre-First World War picture houses tended to be fairly primitive but by the thirties they were building cinemas of the highest quality. In 1932, George Singleton commissioned three new cinemas from James McKissack, the Dundee and Rutherglen Vogues and the innovative **Commodore** in Scotstoun. Built on the site of the old Palladium and opened with the classy *Shanghai Express* (starring

117

Marlene Dietrich and Clive Brook) on 1 January 1933, the Commodore's nautical name and styling reflected the maritime traditions of the home of the Connell and Barclay Curle shipyards. Arguably one of the first moderne-style cinemas in Britain it was praised in *Ideal Kinema* magazine for its appearance of 'strength and dignity without being in the slightest degree austere'. The striking facade was patterned with green, pink and cream faience tiles; horizontal bands up to door-top level then, above the canopy, cheerful vertical stripes around the imposing twin towers. The foyer had a single concealed lighting trough above a bas-relief of stylised sailing ships and the auditorium was simply decorated with curving forms and bas-relief work on the walls. George Singleton had a philosophy about cinema decoration:

> We never felt that ornate decoration was needed because we always started the films before the audience was allowed in. That trick also saved putting the house lights on and spared electricity. In that respect, our cinemas were ahead of their time, for it became normal practice to do simple interiors later in the thirties.

The Singletons may have been frugal with electricity but the Commodore was distinguished from its somewhat tatty neighbours by always being well maintained and smartly run.

The Commodore, Scotstoun, in the 1930s. (Scottish Film Archive)

When the Singleton circuit was sold to Oscar Deutsch in 1936 the Commodore was renamed the **Odeon**. It remained open into the sixties by which time business was slack. A small fire in November 1967 destroyed some seating in the stalls giving Odeon a reason to close it. Sadly it was demolished in the late seventies.

Knightswood – *The Boulevard*

Knightswood, on Glasgow's western fringe was an area of farms, fire-clay pits and coal mines before the thirties, when it became the site of a substantial Corporation housing scheme of flats and semi-detached villas, masterminded by the redoubtable George Smith. Despite Smith's cinema interests it was William Beresford Inglis who opened the **Boulevard** in Knightswood in 1928. The Boulevard was Glasgow's first and most elaborate 'atmospheric' cinema, an intricate essay in Inglis's favourite Spanish-American style.

The Boulevard occupied a spacious site, its entrance facing onto Knightscliffe Avenue with a long side elevation flanking Great Western Road, and was entirely clad in white stucco. There were stubby, pantile-roofed towers at each of the four corners and a mixture of tiling, stuccowork and hacienda windows adorned the frontage. Although the style was dubious, the building had sufficient visual integrity to establish Inglis as an important, if unprolific, cinema architect.

The interior was a great piece of escapism. A glorious Hollywood Andalusian courtyard in a Glasgow housing estate. Either side of the proscenium exotic buildings with stained glass windows, ornamental balconies, fancy wall lanterns and pantiled roofs were massed high to the powder blue sky of the ceiling. It made a spectacular setting for Westerns.

In 1938, the Boulevard was sold to the Singletons. According to George Singleton:

> Inglis said he found running cinemas too stressful and wanted to concentrate on hotels. He complained about film renters, booking agents and problems with staff. Poor man! He seemed unaware that if anything hotels were even worse. Think of the laundry for a start!

Inglis's flagship hotel, the Beresford in Sauchiehall Street, opened in 1938 and, for the Singletons, who had disposed of their previous

119

The Boulevard as Vogue in the 1950s. (Strathclyde Regional Archives)

A section showing the fantastic atmospheric decoration of the Boulevard.

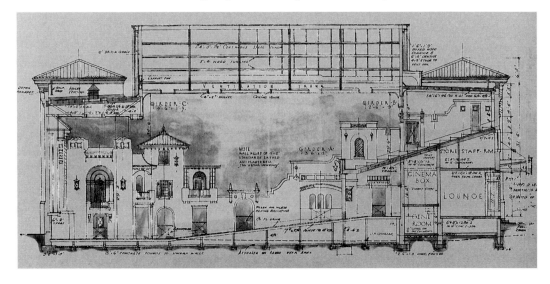

circuit to Odeon, the Boulevard marked a welcome return to the cinema business.

'Atmospheric' cinemas were a product of the silent film era and the arrival of talkies caused them some problems. The Boulevard's audi-

torium had unpredictable acoustics, plaster buildings caused trouble-
some echoes and bounces, so the Singletons commissioned James
McKissack to modernise it. With the seating capacity raised to almost
1,500 and the interior ornamentation removed to create smooth side
walls tapering towards the screen it was re-opened as the **Vogue** in
February 1939. Initially it had a warm reception but, in the fifties it
suffered from the same problems as other cinemas on the urban fringe.
For six months in 1959 its readograph stated 'Closed for Decoration',
but it never reopened and was later demolished. The site is now the
car park for a B&Q store.

Anniesland

Anniesland's first cinema, the humble **Temple Hall** in Fulton Street,
where a Mr A. Wardrop showed films from 1917 until 1924, had been
long closed when, in the late thirties, the district began to resemble a
North London garden suburb. In 1938 two eleven-storey, art deco
style apartment blocks appeared on Great Western Road offering, to
those who could afford it, gracious living, with servants quarters, lifts
and a central laundry. They were soon complemented by an equally
avant-garde cinema just across the road.

The last West End cinema, indeed the last cinema in Scotland, to be
built before the Second World War, the **Ascot** was a brave flourish of
optimism in the face of the worsening political situation in Europe. It
stands at the pinnacle of Scottish cinema architecture, the ultimate
suburban super. The most obvious influence in Charles McNair's
design was the Palace of Industries at the 1938 Empire Exhibition; the
massing and streamlining of the whole structure displaying the
panache that was the hallmark of that event. In the massive, cream-
tiled frontage five tall windows separated by slim, dark-tiled mullions
and flanked by drum-like towers, soared above the great sweeping
canopy, carrying the eye to the angular neon name sign. The windows
lit a double level entrance hall with a geometric-patterned terrazzo
floor and statues set in canopied wall niches either end. The towers
contained sweeping staircases with wave-like balustrades leading to
the auditorium. The 1,900 seat auditorium was suffused with constantly changing coloured light from a series of back-lit coves and the
satin stage curtains in the huge, gently curving proscenium were sepa-
rately lit from above and below. More illuminated coving swept round
the ceiling and rows of scalloped light fittings below the balcony
enhanced the lavish effects.

The outstanding Ascot, Anniesland, pictured in February 1940. It is now used for bingo and disfigured by a huge illuminated sign. (Strathclyde Regional Archives).

The war started during construction so special permission became necessary to complete an amended design but the Ascot was opened on 6 December 1939 with Gracie Fields in *Shipyard Sally*. The theme song, 'Wish Me Luck As You Wave Me Goodbye' was a poignant accompaniment to mobilisation. The Ascot's roof, specially strengthened with extra trusses, was supposedly blast proof and plenty of exits were provided to enable the auditorium to be evacuated quickly. When an air raid siren sounded, the projectionist had to put a red slide over the film and patrons had the choice of hurrying to a shelter or staying in the cinema. When the all-clear sounded, a green slide was displayed. Mercifully, none of Glasgow's cinemas were bombed.

The Ascot was sold to Gaumont in 1943, survived the war unscathed and was re-named **Gaumont** in 1950. Throughout the fifties its popularity never waned. Provost Ian Miller of Bearsden, a film enthusiast, recalls that:

It was a simply wonderful cinema, fully air-conditioned, with bigger seats and more spacious aisles than at the Boulevard out Great Western Road, and thick, lush carpets. All this was reflected in the higher prices; 9d at the Gaumont, only 5d at the

122

Boulevard. The Gaumont also had the best kids' club in the area, much better than the ABC minors at the Grosvenor. The manager, who was known to us kids as Uncle Frank, and his wife, Auntie Bessie, encouraged us to cheer loudly at the right bits. We also sang the Gaumont song:

> 'Every Saturday we come along wearing a smile,
> Every Saturday we come along knowing it's all worthwhile,
> As members of the Gaumont British Club we long to be
> Good citizens and grow up champions of the free!'

When the ritual was over, the youngsters were shown cartoons and Lone Ranger films. West End children's shows tended to be sedate compared to the rowdy shenanigans in the less salubrious halls along Dumbarton Road; the Anniesland children might chatter but fights and spitting were unheard of. 'As the lights dimmed in sequence from the rear to the front and the curtains opened, a hush would fall on the previously noisy youngsters. There was a perceptible tingle of excitement which you rarely experience in any building nowadays. It was all so beautiful!'

In 1964 Rank stopped using the name Gaumont and the Anniesland Gaumont became the **Odeon**. Few takeovers suited the group's corporate image so well and the Odeon traded successfully as a cinema for more than a decade before it closed in October 1975. Owen Monachan, its last manager, put it down to people preferring to see the latest films in the city centre. Thankfully the building survived and is now listed but, surveying the peeling paint and tasteless signage of the County Bingo Club it is difficult to appreciate that this was one of Glasgow's most glamorous picture houses.

The North
Cowcaddens to
Bearsden

Cowcaddens, Woodlands, Woodside and Maryhill Road

The Cowcaddens, what name could be more evocative of Glasgow's teeming, rumbustious past? Before the Second World War the Cowcaddens was characterised by grimy, shop-lined tenement streets and small factories. Tramcars rattled along the main thoroughfares bound for Dalmuir West, Maryhill and Possil and heavily-laden, horse-drawn carts struggled up the hill to Port Dundas on the Forth and Clyde canal. The district's character, however, has changed out of all recognition in the past thirty years. Not only has almost all the old housing been demolished and replaced by high-rise blocks and maisonette flats, but two of its busiest streets, New City Road and Parliamentary Road, have vanished under motorway developments.

To the north west of Cowcaddens, Woodside straddles the Glasgow end of Maryhill Road, bounded to the north by Garscube Road and to the south by Great Western Road. On the fringe of the West End and not quite in the city centre it has always mixed a little of the respectability of the former with the bustling quality of the latter. Perhaps because of its location the Cowcaddens/Woodside area attracted a large number of cinemas in the early days

Maryhill Road was, until the sixties, one of Glasgow's busiest arteries. Long stretches of it were lined with bleak tenements, many of them teeming slums but it was also known for its unusual shops, local characters and close-knit community. Like the other busy arterial roads it had its fair share of picture houses. Redevelopment drastically reduced its population and damaged its individuality. The clattering tramcars vanished, many shops closed and large areas of the old street were torn down. The cinemas went with them.

Early in 1908, following up his success with Pringle's Picture Palace near Glasgow Cross, Ralph Pringle converted the Alexander Assembly

Halls in Cowcaddens Street into the 700 seat **Bijou Picture Palace**. Nicknamed the 'By Jove', it had a narrow entrance up a stair, not ideal for quick exits. In 1929, after a fire alarm at the Glen cinema in Paisley ended in a fatal stampede, the Bijou was closed down for safety reasons.

George Urie Scott's **Electric Picture Palace**, on Maryhill Road near St George's Cross, opened in 1910. The 'Wee Electric' was never the finest of cinemas, and certainly no 'palace'; more a corrugated iron shed squeezed into a tiny triangular back court and entered through a shop. After buying their tickets, customers were ushered into the vestibule, where a black curtain hung over the entrance to the auditorium. It became a joke that a quick dash past this obstacle was necessary to avoid being showered with dust and fleas. Most of the 600 seats were wooden benches and the screen was tobacco-brown. Anyone who missed a big Hollywood film during its first release could come to the 'Wee Electric' months later and see it, with another feature, cartoons, a newsreel, documentaries and a comedy for good measure. The Electric Picture Palace was closed in 1950 but its entrance can still be identified as the front of a picture-framer's shop.

Cinemas were soon appearing all over the district. Between 1910 and 1913 a moving picture show shared the bill with amateur variety acts at the Wilton Halls in Napiershall Street in a venture called the **Empire Electric**. In 1911 a workshop in Hopehill Road was converted into the 350 seat **Sun Picture House** which ran until 1915 and, from 1913 right through to 1931, a simple cinema show called the **Empire Eragraph** operated in the North Woodside Halls in Raglan Street.

John Smith's recollections from the twenties of the **Star** (set up in 1912 in the Garscube Halls, down an alley at 245 Garscube Road) probably apply to many of these early picture houses:

> The 'Starry' was grim. The films were almost as outdated as the pungent, gas-lit hall. The benches were wooden and a few older customers would bring along cushions to ease their backsides. The aisles were covered with tobacco ash and the smells of pipe smoke, gas and disinfectant could be overpowering. We went for the Laurel and Hardy or Buster Keaton comedies and the cartoons. A pianist of sorts bashed away at an out of tune piano. It was great fun!

Among these early developments, the **Zoo Electric Theatre**, was unique. The showman E.H. Bostock ran a huge entertainment complex in New City Road which included an indoor zoo, a circus and a display of grotesques. Writing in 1937, Bostock claimed to have been one of the first film exhibitors in Glasgow:

> I ran films as a sideshow from July 1897 onwards and, that winter, I showed them in the circus as part of my programme. At Christmas 1898, I presented a beautiful picture, *Cinderella*, hand coloured in Paris, and in August 1901, I exhibited the first fight film in the city, *Fitzsimmons v Jeffries*, which was a very big success.

But it was not until January 1911 that he fitted a permanent cinema into his complex. The Zoo Electric Theatre only operated until that September, when the whole place was closed for redevelopment, but it was back in business in December as the **Joytown Grand Electric Theatre**. Bostock claimed that his amusement centre was 'the cheapest attraction in the civilised world' but, though the film shows were inexpensive, they were not enduring, and the cinema's short career ended in October 1918.

The **West End Playhouse**, on St George's Road, was first and foremost a theatre, but it subsidised its plays and variety bills from the proceeds of cinema shows. The stylish, three-tiered hall started its troubled career in August 1913, to close only six months later when its owner, Harry McKelvie, went bankrupt. It opened again, in March 1914, as the **Empress Variety and Picture Playhouse** and the mouthful of a name was reduced to **New Empress** in 1933 when George Urie Scott took over its management. Scott was very proud of the New Empress, whose elegant, red sandstone, Louis XV exterior contrasted sharply with the scruffy 'Wee Electric' only a stone's throw away. But,

St George's Cross with the Empress Theatre and 'Standard' tramcars in the mid 1950s.

despite its elegance, Scott and subsequent owners struggled to make it pay. In 1960 it was sold to the Falcon Trust and renamed the Falcon Theatre and, in June 1962 Alex Frutin bought it as a replacement for his burned out Metropole Music Hall in Stockwell Street, calling it the New Metropole. Jimmy Logan, the popular comedian and actor, paid £80,000 for it in May 1964 as a base for a scheme to revive the great days of Scottish music hall and variety theatre, but this also failed and in 1972 the building was boarded up to spend the next fifteen years becoming increasingly derelict. Ironically, it was demolished in 1988 only a few years before Glasgow became European City of Culture and needed all the theatre space it could find.

The New Grand, Cowcaddens, in the mid 1930s.

The **New Grand Picture House** in Cowcaddens Street was the successor of a line of music halls in a building whose history illustrates how big a problem fire was for theatres and cinemas before strict regulations were introduced. The Prince of Wales was opened in 1867 and two years later lay in ruins after a devastating blaze. It was replaced by a colossal, four-tiered theatre with a reputed capacity of around 4,000 (with no amplification it was little wonder the news-

127

papers reported that it was difficult to hear the acts from the upper reaches of the gallery!). In 1881 this monster closed to re-open as the Grand which, over many years established a worthy tradition of drama and pantomime. In 1909 it was taken over by Moss's Empires, Britain's foremost national theatre chain, who, in 1915, added film shows to the variety programmes. In the same year, fire reduced the building to a twisted shell, out of which the more modestly sized New Grand Picture House emerged. Another rebuild in 1926 introduced a cheerful, jazz-moderne decor in a vivid mix of orange, red, cream, blue and silver. Mrs Ena Macintosh remembers going to the New Grand in the thirties:

> The place stood next door to Dallas's Warehouse, a popular discount department store. When you went inside there was a long narrow hallway with film posters down either side. It was very dark but the auditorium was well lit with bright lighting effects. It was a clean, well run cinema but nothing fancy, just leather seats. You had to be careful to sit near the front because the screen was so wee.

If you didn't feel like sitting there were spacious standing areas too. The New Grand was closed in 1959 to become an extension to Dallas's Warehouse and the whole area disappeared under a comprehensive redevelopment in the late sixties.

With so much cinema activity in the area, it would be surprising if the redoubtable A.E. Pickard did not make an appearance somewhere. Sure enough he did, with the **Seamore**, a huge, strangely windowless and featureless building on a prominent site where North Woodside Road meets Maryhill Road. Just before Christmas 1914, newspaper advertisements announced it as 'Pickard's Masterpiece and the greatest achievement in popular entertainment', showing 'immaculately perfect and indescribably beautiful' films supported by Bert Grapho in a musical revue called *Hullo Maryhill*! The ever optimistic Pickard arranged for special constables to control the crowds he expected on opening night. It was in fact very well attended and the programme played to rapturous applause.

Pickard's eccentricities ensured that the Seamore was never a dull place. It was rebuilt in 1926 with a revolving windmill, illuminated at night with coloured light bulbs, on the roof. Pickard's answer to the Moulin Rouge! He claimed that a large clock mounted high on the Seamore's facade kept perfect time, offering a reward of £1 to anyone who could prove that it deviated by more than two seconds from Greenwich Mean Time. Inside the auditorium a series of ceiling paintings of female nudes in various shapes and sizes substantiated his slogan 'You'll see more at the Seamore!' He refused at first to fit talkie apparatus, preferring to engage variety acts to accompany his dated silent films, even encouraging the usherettes to sing and dance as one of the acts!

In 1932 the Seamore expanded into the tenement building next door, increasing the seating capacity to over two thousand, and a lift was installed to carry customers up to the circle. Then, in 1935, Pickard sold it, with the rest of his circuit, to A.B. King. King renovated it, dismantled the windmill, obliterated the nudes and introduced talkies. King's promotional gimmicks were a bit less flamboyant than Pickard's – the highlight of the Seamore's years before the Second World War was the Novelty Night at Hogmanay when the children in the audience were given a small gift (usually something which made a lot of noise) – but tended to be more successful.

The Seamore had a fan-shaped auditorium and an exceptionally wide proscenium which made it ideal for CinemaScope and, in December 1953, it became the first cinema in the area to fit the new system. Mrs Anne Menzies remembers seeing *The Robe* there:

> We sat ourselves right in the middle of the stalls. The place was packed. At last the lights went down and the curtains opened to what looked like just the normal distance. 'Disnae look awfie big to me', said a woman somewhere behind. Then they opened wider and wider to reveal a screen three times as big as normal. The 20th Century Fox sign and music came on and a voice announced, 'Ladies and Gentlemen, this is CinemaScope!' We were on the edge of our seats and there was a collective 'Ooh' from the audience. It was one of my favourite experiences in years of going to the pictures.

In the mid fifties, the Seamore was one of four run-down cinemas in the north of Glasgow bought up by J. Arthur Rank's Circuits Management Association as property speculation, but it stayed in business until 1963 and then lay derelict for several years before a fire destroyed it. Ironically, A.E. Pickard used to joke about the Seamore, which he never insured, 'I built the place, so I knew it would never burn down'.

A.E. Pickard was rarely out of the public eye for long. In 1951 he stood for Parliament as Maryhill's 'Millionaire Candidate' with the campaign slogan: 'Some men enter politics because they are too lazy to work. Pickard enters politics because he has never worked in his life.' The whole thing was a publicity stunt designed to outdo his longstanding rival E.H. Bostock, who had earlier been elected a Glasgow Corporation councillor. Not surprisingly he only got 351 votes and lost his deposit.

The **Granville Cinema,** on Great Western Road, near St George's Cross, started life in 1921 as the Windsor Hall of the North West Wesleyan Mission. When talkies came along the small hall was thoroughly rebuilt, given a balcony and re-opened in 1928 as the **Gem.** A curvaceous canopy and fin-shaped name sign made from cream and pale green vitrolite, a novel and quintessentially thirties material, were installed on the face of the soot-blackened tenement. James McPhie, a vitrolite supplier, had showrooms nearby and several shop fronts in the vicinity had signs made of the opaque, glassy sheeting. The Gem's long, narrow hallway led to a bright, jazz-moderne auditorium with skyscraper murals and zig-zag motifs on the side walls. The accommodation ranged from couch seats in the rear balcony for courting couples to a standee area behind the stalls, which was particularly busy on wet days. The Gem closed in 1958 and the gutted building was a car showroom until the eighties. Flats have since been built on the site.

The **Phoenix** also opened in 1921, just off Garscube Road. It became a minor member of the ABC circuit in 1928 and was sold, in 1943, to an independent exhibitor. Mr N. Herring, a regular visitor to the Phoenix during the Second World War, recalls how primitive its projection technology was even then:

> If I didn't have my Saturday penny, I could always get in by handing over a jam jar at the pay-box and on one occasion I was even allowed into the projection room where I was shown how the equipment worked. They didn't have incandescent bulbs. There were two carbon rods, held about three-eighths of an inch apart, and a spark jumped the gap. The resulting arc threw a flickering image onto the screen. Occasionally the projectionist had to stop the film to replace the rods, which slowly burned away and required constant adjustment to maintain the spark.

The Phoenix operated as the **Endrick** from December 1948 until 1955 when it was closed and used as a warehouse before being demolished in 1972.

1922 saw the appearance of another two new cinemas. The **Cambridge** in New City Road was a clever conversion from a United Presbyterian Church. It had a handsome classical frontage, but the hall itself was rudimentary and even a thorough reconstruction in 1927 under the direction of Charles McNair left the auditorium unadorned. By contrast, the very downmarket **Grafton,** in Parliamentary Road, was not even free-standing but relied on the tenement block in front of it for support. It showed revivals of old films,

remembered mainly for how worn the prints were, in a poky, dirty auditorium. Both were swept away when Parliamentary Road and large sections of New City Road were bulldozed to build the M8.

The **Blythswood**, like the Seamore, occupied a prominent corner site on Maryhill Road, in this case at the junction with Trossachs Street. Opened in 1927 it was kite-shaped in plan, one plain, rough-cast flank running down each street from a modest, tiled entrance portico at the apex. The small auditorium was also plain, but comfortable and cosy, with twenty rows of 'dear seats' set just four steps up from the stalls. Though privately run, the Blythswood showed the best films available. Mrs Menzies remembers its heyday:

> There were lots of musicals such as *Broadway Melody* and great gangster movies; Bogart, Cagney and George Raft were our favourites. We all thought that Barbara Stanwyck was 'a rare wee greeter'. Half the audience were in tears too. Then there were cartoons with the words of the latest hit songs. A little white ball bounced from word to word in time to the music and folk would sing along with great gusto.

The Cambridge, located amid the decaying tenements of New City Road. (Caledonian Newspapers)

The Blythswood as a bingo hall in the 1970s. (Chris Doak)

Stars visited the Blythswood, notably, in February 1954, Roy Rogers and his horse Trigger, children's favourite cowboy heroes. Crowds blocked the roads and halted the tramcars outside the Blythswood; it seemed as though everyone in Maryhill Road had come to see them. Both man and horse stayed in the opulent Central Station Hotel where Trigger must have caused the management some concern as he was paraded round the foyer for the benefit of the Press.

The Blythswood was the last cinema still operating in the area when it was turned over to bingo in 1972. The bingo sessions ended in 1978 and the Blythswood was demolished.

A.E. Pickard was not one to be deterred by much. Even the arrival of the big city centre supers did not put him off planning a replacement for his ageing Panopticon. In 1936, two years before the Panopticon closed, he opened the **Norwood** on St George's Road just south of St George's Cross on the edge of the city centre. The stadium-type hall was actually a comprehensive conversion of the Norwood Ballroom, but Pickard told his customers that it had been specially designed without steps to allow disabled access! Both externally and internally the Norwood in its heyday must have been an extraordinary sight. Above the canopy Pickard recreated two cantilevers modelled on the Forth Railway Bridge. Worse still, he had the entire auditorium clad in glass and faceted mirrors. The spectacular reflections this caused during film performances must have been very distracting. Local folk dubbed it 'Pickard's Crystal Palace'. A special tapestry,

132

woven by Templeton's carpets, was glued to the ceiling and Pickard's beloved Kilmarnock edition of Burns was displayed in the vestibule.

Pickard himself opened the Norwood unconventionally by charging across St George's Road with a battering ram and breaking the doors open before inviting the onlookers inside. Whether because of its eccentricities or competition from city centre cinemas, the Norwood was never a great success. It was sold in 1945 to George Palmer who renamed it the **George** and had his initials applied in mosaic tiles throughout the interior. Palmer removed the mirrors from the auditorium but the Forth Bridge replica stayed until ABC bought the George in 1955 to replace the old King's in Sauchiehall Street as their second-run hall. In 1975 it became **Dreamland**, an Asian cinema serving the area's Pakistani community. It is now a snooker club.

The Maryhill Road cinemas weren't all at the city end. Much further along, at number 1046, the **Star** opened for business in 1912. It was rebuilt several times, extending further and further into the back court of the surrounding tenements and a comprehensive reconstruction in 1931 included the installation of a wide screen and a change of name. The **New Star**'s big corrugated steel roof amplified the sound track so effectively that it could be heard far along Maryhill Road. The wide screen was not fully used until the fifties when CinemaScope had a brief innings at the New Star. Sadly, through the fifties and into

The New Star.
(Dr C.P. Stewart)

133

the sixties the auditorium declined into squalor and the New Star closed in 1966 to be used as a car showroom until that part of the road was redeveloped in the mid-seventies.

The little-known **Maryhill Picture House** operated between 1914 and 1929 on a site that had once been a washing green and, on the same site, the legendary **Roxy** opened in 1935. 'Roxy' was the nickname of Samuel Rothafel, the flamboyant showman manager of the Radio City Music Hall and the Roxy cinema in New York City, the world's biggest and grandest movie theatre. The latter's Maryhill namesake was certainly the area's biggest cinema, but there the similarity ended. Designed by Lennox and McMath, the Maryhill Roxy was simply a big barn; though its pretentious twin-towered facade stood out in an otherwise undistinguished streetscape, it had few aspirations to metropolitan splendour. It was operated by James Graham, whose circuit consisted mainly of lower end of the market cinemas in industrial neighbourhoods and, in fairness, it was far from the worst of these. It seated over two thousand and the best seats were rattan couches with plush red cushions set into niches in the slips of the huge horseshoe-shaped balcony. Variety programmes originally

The Roxy, taken in the 1930s. (Strathclyde Regional Archives)

complemented the films at the Roxy, but other kinds of fun and games often distracted the audience. Once the lights dimmed, youngsters would make surreptitiously for the toilets, not for the usual reason but to open the fire escapes to let their friends in without paying. Soldiers from the Highland Light Infantry barracks at nearby Wyndford were frequent customers (particularly for the one shilling couches where they liked to entertain their girlfriends) and audience participation was often lively. The highlight of the week was the Thursday night talent contest when young (and not so young) hopefuls risked all, enduring muttered comments or yells of encouragement from the soldiery for meagre half-crown prizes.

As people tried to escape the worries of the Second World War and relax in warmth and relative security, cinemas were busy seven days a week, catering specially for the Forces on Sundays. By the end of the war the Roxy was badly dilapidated. 'Girlie' films began to be screened for the large numbers of demobbed soldiers and things went from bad to worse. In 1955 the Roxy was one of the cinemas bought in Rank's site speculation but it remained standing until 1962 when it was demolished, along with the surrounding run-down tenements, to make way for a community shopping development and a pub.

Maryhill Road leads beyond the Glasgow City boundary to Bearsden and Milngavie, the former of which saw one of the first film shows in Scotland, given by the Bearsden Literary Society in the local Free Church (now Bearsden North Parish Church) in October 1896. At that time the village did not have electricity and the show was given with limelight and a hand-cranked projector. The area had to wait until 1934 before it had a proper cinema.

The **Rio** at Canniesburn Toll was built to a tight budget, part of which was won on the football pools. The construction was utilitarian, but inside it was spacious, well-lit, clean and comfortable with an auditorium decorated in red plush with gold and cream moderne detailing. It was a cut above its nearest rival, the Maryhill Roxy, and in its early years, advertised as 'The Family House', it prospered. It was bought in 1936 by a Perthshire-based company who sold it, in 1938, to CAC's Scottish Central Cinemas, under whose management it had a long and successful career. Catering to changing trends in cinema-going, it was 'twinned' in 1975. The structure would not stand elaborate reconstruction and money was tight, so the stalls were divided in two very economically; so much so that there was no sound insulation and subsequently the galloping horses and shooting from a cowboy movie often intruded on the amorous embraces of a heart-throb romance next door. CAC sold the Rio to property developers in 1986 and an uninspiring block of flats now occupies the site.

Possil

Possil's coal and ironstone deposits made it a focus for metalworking, notably in Walter MacFarlane's Saracen Foundry which produced cast iron goods. MacFarlane's often exotic products, ranging from bandstands to urinals, ornamented the townscapes of nineteenth century Scotland and found their way all over the British Empire. Smaller firms, such as Robert J. Smith's which specialised in canopies, railings and other paraphernalia for theatres and cinemas, also prospered.

Possil was characterised by narrow streets of tenements until, in the thirties, Glasgow Corporation built a huge new housing scheme there. Successful at first, this became a social and economic black spot with high unemployment and its attendant poverty and degradation.

The white painted frontage of **Green's Picturedrome** contrasted strikingly with the dull exterior of the Possil tenement building in which it opened in 1912. The Greens leased it in 1920 to operators who renamed it the **Round Toll Cinema** and it did well until 1931 when the threat of competition from the Astoria (see below) scared the tenants off. Things could not have been as bad as anticipated though; renamed the **Magnet** this little 500 seater catered to the lower end of the Possil cinema market for another 24 years before the block of which it was part was erased from the scene. The rough **Possil Park Picture House** also survived super cinema competition for many years. James Graham ran it from 1920 until he sold his whole circuit in 1945 and it continued to operate under private ownership as the **Avon** until 1955. It was then sold to CMA and replaced by a pub in 1960.

Glasgow's second largest cinema (and said to have the biggest balcony in the city), the extraordinary **Astoria**, was more of an engineering marvel than a visual feast. Architect A.V. Gardner's biggest ever project, the fan-shaped building was erected on the massive site of a filled-in quarry on Possil Road. Excavation to a depth of thirty feet was necessary to allow the foundations to stand on solid rock, and the sheer size of this 6,000 square feet, 3,000 seat mammoth meant that it took sixteen months to build – a long time in cinema construction terms. The finished exterior impressed by its scale but not by its elegance. Concrete detailing did little to relieve the monotony of the vast roughcast walls, perforated with prison-like windows and capped with an industrial style asbestos roof, dwarfing a dull two storey

The Astoria, seen when new. (Strathclyde Regional Archives)

entrance portico. Only the huge, bulb-studded name sign, held in mid-air by a temporary-looking metal framework, gave the impression of a place of entertainment.

The interior, by contrast, had a festive air. A contemporary issue of *Building Industries* magazine recorded the original decoration:

> The vestibule is octagonal in shape, as is the box office, which stands in the middle of the space. The colour scheme . . . is very brightly carried out in a variety of browns, mauves and fawns with golden lights. From the entrance hall one sees on the first landing a very effective rising sun motif in gold, green and red . . . . The auditorium decoration is carried out in modified futuristic fashion with a shade of marigold predominating . . . the design of the ceiling is emphasised by four large cubist lights, suspended to form a square and with a huge, brightly coloured inverted cone slung in the centre. The sun decoration is enhanced by grotesque figures on the side walls . . .

The cinema trade press enthusiastically described the Astoria as 'the largest working class sound kinema in the world' and Sir Robert Wilson, performing the opening ceremony on 2 February 1931,

137

praised A.B. King and the other directors for having 'erected a temple which goes far to adorn the somewhat sombre streets of this area'. The cheerful interior and good quality films and variety programmes, supported for many years by an orchestra, attracted big audiences. The Astoria's popularity was apparently unaffected when the variety acts were abandoned in 1938 but, by 1955, attendances had dwindled badly; it was closed and sold to Rank, to re-open in 1962 as the Top Rank Club, one of Glasgow's earliest bingo halls. It remained opened for bingo, with corrugated metal sheets covering the entrance portico and the already depressing exterior deteriorating steadily, until March 1995, shortly after which it was knocked down.

Many Glasgow cinemas ended their careers under the name 'Mecca', but one actually started life that way. The **Mecca Picture House** in Balmore Road was built in 1933, to an imposing design by James McKissack, to serve the new Corporation housing estate. Its owners were George Smith and James Welsh, whose fine cinemas graced so many suburban housing developments. On a prominent corner site, its three-faced frontage was clad up to door-top level with bands of buff and cream tiles framing brass-handled, glass doors and moderne stained-glass windows. Above the big canopy rose an angular, red sandstone facade topped by a prominent red name sign, all, originally, vividly outlined with red, green and blue neon zig-zags. The jazz-moderne idiom was continued inside where the foyer, though cramped, was decorated with brightly-painted plasterwork and elegant wooden dados. James Welsh rightly believed that patrons would seldom see the inside of his cinemas with the house lights on and insisted that McKissack concentrate the decoration around the proscenium. Consequently, the internal treatment of the Mecca still looks remarkably modern. The auditorium was illuminated from side wall niches covered in glass acid-etched with moderne patterns and there was a simple covered proscenium arch with flood-lit curtains.

The Mecca passed, with other Smith and Welsh picture houses, to George Singleton in January 1950 and shortly thereafter became the **Vogue**. It became a bingo hall in 1968 and was operated until recently by the Singletons. The opening of a purpose built bingo hall nearby might have finished the Vogue but it was attractively refurbished and fought back, attracting an older clientele who appreciate its distinctive 'picture house' atmosphere.

Springburn

Springburn used to mean railways. With the Caledonian Railway's St Rollox works, the North British Railway's Cowlairs works and the mighty North British Locomotive Company's works at Hyde Park the district was the greatest centre of locomotive and railway engineering in the world. Springburn-built locomotives ran on every inhabited continent and Springburn folk had plenty of reasons to be proud of their achievements. This kind of engineering was highly skilled but heavy, dirty and often dangerous work from which going to the pictures was a welcome break. Though the city centre was only a penny tram ride away, Springburn, like many other industrial districts, had a quite extraordinary number of local cinemas.

Springburn's first film shows were given in the impressive, red-sandstone Public Hall, but the first true cinema was the **Springburn Electric Theatre**, a real 'bug hut' entered up a close in Springburn Road. Opened in 1911, it was a former meeting hall whose roof completely filled the back court and which had seats for about 500 with a so-called 'gallery' only two steps up from the 'stalls'. It was so murky that children were able to hide in women's long skirts and sneak past the doorman without paying. Renamed the **Ideal Picture House** in 1916, it was anything but ideal. Around that time the twice nightly entertainment consisted of silent films and variety acts. Pity the entertainers who had to get ready in the 'dressing room', just a curtain hung behind the pianist, to perform on a stage only a few planks wide. The three-piece band played only a few feet away from the front row and the rowdy audiences enjoyed throwing missiles to distract the musicians; the trumpet horn and the band leader's bald head were favourite targets.

The 'wee Ideal' belonged to Mrs Stockwell, the wife of the manager of the glamorous La Scala in Sauchiehall Street; the Stockwells lived in Gourlay Street, just round the corner from the cinema. In 1925 it was renamed the **Royal** and promoted with a series of odd publicity stunts. When the film *Cocaine* was showing, two Chinese men stood by the pay-box handing out sachets of white powder; luckily it was only flour. On another occasion a tall man in Red Indian costume invited children to grab his long hair by which he lifted them off the floor. His partner was an escapologist called Atlanta who allowed herself to be handcuffed by the local policeman and tied into a sack, from which she always managed to release herself, panting and red in the face. The Royal's owners could not afford talkie apparatus and it closed in 1930. It subsequently housed shops, then a billiard hall and, from 1961 until the mid seventies, a Prize bingo club.

Just a few doors along Springburn Road from the Electric, the **Canadian Picture House** opened in 1912. A poor conversion from a Baptist church, the draughty, wooden-framed hall was clad in corrugated iron and nicknamed 'Tin Heaven' by picture-goers who froze in winter and roasted on hot summer days. Saturday matinees, known as 'the penny crush', were packed with tough kids and at the romantic scenes shouts like 'come oan, gie ur a kiss and get it ower wi!' were common. When the audience got too unruly the attendant would select someone with the beam of his torch to be ejected unceremoniously as an example to the rest. These 'victims' became heroes after the show, encouraging further carry-ons the following week.

The 'Tin Heaven' was torn down in 1925 and replaced by a new, roughcast brick building with a neon signboard above the doors proclaiming it as the **Kinema**. Perhaps A.V. Gardner's most unusual cinema design, it was nicknamed 'The Coffin' because of its strange shape and proximity to Sighthill Cemetery. It was also known as 'The Ranch' because it always seemed to be showing ancient cowboy films. Though ugly, grey and weather-stained, the Kinema's well-planned interior made the best use of an odd sloping site. The separate entrances for the front and rear stalls were at street level, from which narrow flights of stairs led up to an 850 seat, stadium-plan auditorium with pilastered side walls and a small, square screen set into a narrow proscenium. Since the Kinema pre-dated talkies there was a small stage and orchestra pit. Though downmarket, it never accepted jam jars for admission but Tom Weir, the mountaineer and author, who once played the drums in the Kinema's band, remembers an even cheaper way to see the films:

> There was a big telegraph pole outside the front . . . My wee brother used to climb that because you could see the film through a ventilator in the side. He was only found out because he got so excited at one point that he forgot to hold on and fell off and broke his elbow.

Springburn folk liked to show off their special knowledge and, when a silent train raced through canyons and careered over frail bridges with the agitated hero clinging on for dear life, a gruff voice from the back might mutter, 'Fur Christ's sake, can ye no pit oan the bloody brake?'

The Kinema was sold to the Greens in 1954 but closed and demolished in 1958.

The **Prince's**, which opened in Gourlay Street in 1914, was probably the first cinema to be run by John Maxwell. Behind a symmetrical,

The first Prince's Cinema in Gourlay St.

twin-towered show-facade typical of the period, the original 998 seat hall presented cine-variety until the mid twenties. Harry Houdini, the celebrated magician and escapologist, once attracted such huge crowds there that he had to perform on the entrance steps to satisfy them all. Mrs Marion Smith recalls that it was also used for political rallies:

> As well as being our favourite cinema, Springburn folk were privileged to hear such political giants as Jimmy Maxton, Manny Shinwell and George Hardie (half-brother of Keir Hardie) at the Prince's. We stood in our hundreds outside in the street and waited for the election results to come through. They shouted them from the steps of the Prince's. The enthusiasm for the socialist cause was terrific in those days.

Another giant seen regularly at the Prince's was its commissionaire, Big Rab Horner. Rab laboured by day in Cowlairs railway works and supervised the queues at the picture house in the evenings, proudly sporting a splendid, long, double-breasted, brass-buttoned coat trimmed with gold piping and his grimy working bunnet, which he never took off.

In November 1937 ABC replaced the Prince's with a new cinema on the same site. The frontage was unusually stark for a McNair designed

141

Gourlay Street with the second Prince's cinema in the 1960s. (Springburn Museum)

ABC cinema but concealed a comfortable, attractive 2,000 seat 'super' auditorium. It opened with *After the Thin Man*, starring William Powell and Myrna Loy, and often shared programmes with ABC's other super in a working class suburb, the Govan Plaza. It was well used by the robust locals and by the sixties the carpets, seats and other fittings were worn out. It closed in July 1968 with a double bill of *Helicopter Spies* and *The Fastest Gun Alive*. From June 1969 Star Leisure leased the Prince's for bingo which EMI, the new owners of ABC, then ran as part of a social club from 1975 until 1979 when most of the old Gourlay Street buildings were demolished.

The **Springburn Picture House**, which stood on the north side of Wellfield Street and was known locally as the 'Wellfield', was a tin shed with an asbestos roof built in 1920 as part of James Graham's rather shoddy circuit. Customers, according to tradition, had jerseys when they went in and jumpers when they came out, but Harry Foster, its manager, did his best to keep up basic standards. He would stride up and down the aisles spraying clouds of disinfectant into the air and, when the audience got too rowdy, would crank the curtains shut and bellow through a loudhailer until order was restored. In 1947 the

142

Springburn's owners held a competition to find a new name for their cinema. 'The Flea's Playground' was a popular nomination but the more salubrious sounding **Astor** won. The new name did little to enhance the condition of the place which was pretty poor when it was sold to Rank's Circuits Management Association in 1955. It was repainted, new seats were installed and it continued to operate until November 1966 when it closed with *Inherit the Wind*. The empty building was gutted by fire and had to be demolished.

In 1927, Bernard Frutin had part of the old tramway workshops in Keppochhill Road ingeniously converted by Lennox and McMath into the **Oxford Playhouse**, a 1,500 seat cinema with full stage facilities. The three tramway arches were retained, the outside ones as windows and the middle one as the main entrance, and a long auditorium, lit from false bay windows, was created with three boxes either side and deep wooden dados at both stalls and balcony levels. Frutin ran high-quality cine-variety shows at the Oxford, often presenting big stars, such as the comedians Tommy Yorke and Tommy Morgan, from his

The Oxford Playhouse: the tramway arches are still evident on the facade.
(Springburn Museum)

Metropole Music Hall in Stockwell Street. A local man, George Marshall, or 'Maestro Marshallato' as he was known, conducted a ten-piece orchestra to accompany the variety acts and silent films. Tragically, on New Year's Day 1941, the Oxford was reduced to a pile of blackened rubble by a fire which took nine hours to put out. With the wartime restrictions on materials it was not rebuilt.

The East End

Townhead

The heart of medieval Glasgow lay around the thirteenth century cathedral and fifteenth century university, the area now known as Townhead. The growing Georgian and Victorian city centre peripheralised Townhead to the extent that, for convenience, we can regard the East End as starting at the medieval High Street. As the city grew, tenements replaced Townhead's cottages with their narrow kail-yards. When the population soared early in the nineteenth century more tenements, the infamous 'backlands', were built in the back courts of existing ones, depriving the surrounding dwellings of light and air. The City Improvements Acts of 1866 and 1897 and other similar legislation were brave early ventures in municipal housing management, but primarily benefited those well-off enough to pay higher rents. Townhead remained a poor, densely populated area in which the cinema provided a welcome escape for the imagination.

In 1907, Ralph Pringle opened **Pringle's Picture Palace**, presenting cine-variety programmes in what had been the Shakespeare Music Hall and later the Queen's Theatre, in Watson Street close to Glasgow Cross. The theatre occupied the top three floors of a warehouse building. In striking contrast to the exterior, the three tiered auditorium was lavishly ornate, with Corinthian columns around the proscenium and Moorish domes over the side boxes. Bernard Frutin leased it in 1914 and continued the cine-variety but it was not particularly well suited to film exhibition and never the success he expected. In 1934 films were abandoned and it became a music hall again until fire destroyed it in 1952.

A small, gas-lit sign by a close mouth at 112 Stirling Street was the only indication of the presence of the **St James's Picture House**, a 450 seat nickelodeon opened in 1910. In its heyday it ran two shows nightly and soldiered on until 1947, when the lease ran out.

A.E. Pickard's **Casino**, opened in 1911, was the first 'proper' cinema in the area. Designed by George Boswell, the Casino had an entrance foyer with a pay-box at each end, one for the stalls and another for the balcony. The 987 seat auditorium had boxes at the rear and the superfluous ferrules and bizarre motifs in its decoration were doubtless to its quirky owner's taste. To celebrate the opening, Pickard personally composed a set of verses to the tune 'Killaloe' and had them printed in the entertainment columns of the Glasgow papers:

> Ach! Now listen to my song, and I won't detain you long,
> It's to tell you of a place you ought to see,
> The CASINO, don't you know, it will be a wonderful show,
> And the opening day's OCTOBER TWENTY THREE.
> Now don't forget the date – for you're going to have a trate –
> For Pickard is the captain of the crew,
> Though he isn't six feet high, HIS FAME HAS REACHED THE SKY,
> As a man with ENTERTAINMENTS BRIGHT AND NEW – Don't talk of
> Bonaparte or dinners à la carte,
> But come and have a laugh and share the treat;
> With sweethearts join the bean-o in PICKARD'S NEW CASINO,
> So come along and join the throng, we're bound for Castle
> Street . . .
> See the Cinematograph, for its bound to make you laugh,
> THE NEWEST PICTURES there you may be sure;
> All the LATEST films will go, whether rain or shine or snow,
> Dr Pickard for all trouble's got the cure.
> The ROYAL 'cross the way will lose patients every day,
> Our professor from the TRON will take the case:
> The CASINO'S TREATMENTS RARE, for it drives away all care,
> Patronise this BENEFACTOR TO THE RACE. Etc. Etc.

The 'Royal' was not a rival cinema but the Glasgow Royal Infirmary, just a stone's throw from the casino, and the 'Tron' was Pickard's own former Panopticon. The publicity effort appears to have been successful. *The Daily Record* of 24 October noted that 'A.E. Pickard's latest venture . . . was given an enthusiastic send off with the house crowded for both the 7pm and 9pm performances'. The films were described as 'bright and steady' and included the 'picture dramas' *The Priestess of Carthage, On a Tramp Steamer* and *The Hands*, each 'of an intensely dramatic nature as well as setting forth humorous incidents'. The variety acts were the 'society entertainers' Healey and Mealey, H.C. Vicars, an actor vocalist, and a comedian called Charles Champney.

In the twenties, Glasgow Casino Ltd (in which A.B. King was involved) bought the Casino from Pickard and the directors were so pleased with their new purchase they held a luncheon in his honour. All was gaiety and merriment until the Chairman rose to his feet and frowned gravely in Pickard's direction. 'I've just had some disturbing news', he announced, 'I've just learned that our guest of honour, Mr Pickard, has bought the ground opposite the Casino.' As the site was perfect for a cinema it is easy to imagine the concern the Casino's new owners must have felt. Pickard was unabashed. 'How sensible it is', he replied 'that the ground which could have been used by the opposition now belongs to a friend of the Casino rather than an enemy.' He later sold the vacant site to the Glasgow Casino Ltd, who in turn sold it to James Graham.

The **Carlton Picture House**, which Graham opened on this site in January 1926, was rather better than the others in his circuit and the 1,600 seat hall, designed by Duff and Cairns, was certainly superior to the old Casino. A domed tower on the corner of Castle Street and busy Alexander Parade proclaimed its presence though the rest of the building was dully clad in grey roughcast. It backed onto a basin on the Monkland Canal and a memorial, raised in 1818 by the Monkland's Canal Company to three Covenanters killed during the

The Casino in the late 1950s.

147

religious persecutions of the seventeenth century, had to be moved to allow its construction. This Martyr's Fountain was preserved and built into one side wall of the Carlton and Graham had T.H. Weir, a local historian, write a book about it. In 1945, the Carlton went with the rest of Graham's circuit to A.B. King and, a decade later, was sold to Rank's Circuit's Management Association. The Casino and the Carlton were close competitors for almost forty years and closed within a year of one another. The Casino became a bingo club in February 1965 but it was unsuccessful and closed permanently in 1968 to be demolished five years later. The Carlton was closed in March 1966 and demolished to make way for the first phase of Glasgow's Inner Ring Road. The Martyr's Fountain disappeared with it but a replica of the inscription on its base was carved on a pier of the nearby motorway flyover. Apart from the Cathedral, Provand's Lordship, the Royal Infirmary and a handful of kirks, old Townhead, like its cinemas, has been largely obliterated.

Calton, Bridgeton and Dalmarnock

At the beginning of the twentieth century, Calton and Bridgeton, known to the locals as 'Brigton', were tough districts whose economy was based around textile mills making everything from carpets to fine cloth for shirts. Their crowded and decaying tenement streets became notorious in the inter-war years as the stamping grounds of violent gangs. There were the Briggate Boys and the Calton Entry, but most notable were the Protestant Billy Boys from Calton and the Catholic Norman Conks from Norman Street in Bridgeton. Much of their time was spent in picture houses and some of their activities were clearly influenced by the movies. But the majority of the area's citizens were as peaceable as anyone else and liked nothing better than a night at the pictures.

Most of the strange assortment of makeshift early cinemas in Bridgeton had short working lives, occasionally succumbing to the strains of poor construction or old age but more often being driven out of business in the late twenties and early thirties by competition from large, purpose built cinemas showing talking films.

In 1908, a Mrs Baird began giving picture shows in the **Star Palace**, a big hall (it could hold over 1,000 people) upstairs in the former Bridgeton Town Hall and **Green's Whitevale Theatre** opened at 845 Gallowgate. In 1910, Richard Singleton leased the Globe Theatre, a rickety music hall in Tobago Street, Calton, which he called the

Paragon Picture House and the nickelodeon-style **Bridgeton Cross Electric Theatre** opened in Olympia Street. From 1912 the latter was operated by George Green as **Green's Picturedrome**; legend has it that it was so filthy the cleaners didn't bother trying to mop the floor but turned a hose on it from a safe distance. These pioneers had all closed by 1932.

Some of the early film exhibitors set up cinemas in any kind of building with enough space, and inauspicious buildings did not necessarily preclude long term success as two other Bridgeton cinemas opened in 1910 indicate. J.J. Bennell's **London Road Picture Palace** had been the Bon Accord Engine Works (the flat floored auditorium didn't appear to have changed very much since) and the **King's Picture Theatre** in James Street was a converted army drill hall which had briefly been used a roller skating rink. The latter was fitted with a sloping floor so that the screen was visible from all 1,300 seats but the front rows were still wooden benches. Both survived as cinemas into the fifties.

Spartan as they were, these early cinemas were often exciting places. Mrs Maidie Cairey recalls the King's in the thirties:

> It was a tough, basic cinema for working class people but that didn't stop the stars from coming to visit. Laurel and Hardy and

A 1950s view of The King's in James Street. The tiled facade dates from a renovation in 1936. (A. Duda Collection)

149

Edward G. Robinson called by, made speeches, signed photos, gave autographs and shook hands. The stars loved to meet their fans in those days. I'm sure it flattered their egos. The queues were just terrific and buskers came along to entertain us. One was a Charlie Chaplin impersonator. He did the wee walk and twirled his cane so well that us weans couldn't tell the difference! There were also variety turns. Sometimes it was a conjuror, sometimes a wee man with a harmonica – really good, down-to-earth fun!

After the First World War a new generation of cinemas appeared in Bridgeton.

The cheapest of these was the **Royal** in Main Street, known familiarly as 'The Wee Royal' or, as a result of the Glaswegian penchant for rhyming slang, 'The Dan Doyle'. Crammed into a back court in 1918, its 500 seats were often filled. It was the favourite for 'penny matinees'. If times were hard two jam jars got you into the cheap seats, which, as usual, were hard wooden benches, but the wily slipped over to the cushioned area under cover of darkness. The Royal's popularity was boosted by the management giving free fruit, sweets or comics to the younger customers.

East of Bridgeton Cross, the **Black Cat**, in Springfield Road, opened in 1921. It was just a free-standing brick shed with a flat floor but, being an A.E. Pickard picture house, it had its own eccentricities. The seats had high plywood backs, according to their promoter, 'specially made to a revolutionary design to keep the bugs away'. The problem was that they were so high people could not see over them and shorter folk often had to stand. It was hardly a recipe for success, but, fitted with more conventional seating, the Black Cat remained in business until 1955 when it was sold to the BBC for use as a television studio. In the sixties, *The White Heather Club*, a popular Scottish song and dance show, starring Andy Stewart, was broadcast from there. It subsequently became a film studio and then a warehouse.

The **Scotia** also opened for business in 1921. Designed by Charles McNair, its rudimentary brick-faced frontage, on Millerston Street, had a bland portico and twin stair towers topped by squat spires. The tall, narrow auditorium filled the back court of tenements on Duke Street and, although there were pilasters on the side walls and ornamental cornices around the ceiling, the exposed roof trusses betrayed the cheap construction. Nor was there anything fancy about the leather-covered benches in the stalls or the humble tip-up seats on the balcony. But, though basic, the Scotia was always popular. In the

thirties, the highpoint of the year was a children's show sponsored by Blochairn Foundry, whose workers were given free passes to 'take hame to the weans'. The manager dished out oranges and pokes of sweeties and the kids were treated to Laurel and Hardy, Charlie Chaplin, Tom Mix Westerns or cartoons. The Scotia was seriously damaged by fire in February 1949 and repairs took almost a year. The much improved interior had a moderne proscenium and what claimed to be the first RCA Synchroscreen installation in Scotland (loudspeakers were fitted behind the screen to make the sound more realistic). Bingo took over in 1964 and was a crowd puller at first but, as the surrounding tenements were cleared, custom declined. Competition from more comfortable Mecca clubs with bigger prize money sealed the Scotia's fate and it closed in 1985. It lay empty until vandals set fire to it in 1987 and it had to be demolished.

The district's grandest cinema not only still survives but the mighty red sandstone facade of the **Olympia** designed by George Arthur still dominates Bridgeton Cross; above the curving corner entrance, ionic columns, and, along the main wall, slim pilasters flanked by rusticated ends, rise over three storeys to a balustraded parapet, surmounted by an imposing dome. Originally the Olympia Theatre of Varieties, the 2,000 seat, two tiered auditorium was decorated with the lush and rather bulbous plaster scrollwork typical of the later work of its architect, Frank Matcham, and painted in two tones of cream with gilded

151

The Olympia as ABC in 1972 showing Clint Eastwood in Dirty Harry. (Ian Cunningham)

ornamentation. In its early days Bridgeton's pride and joy was advertised as 'the clean, comfortable family resort' and was immensely popular with audiences, who could enjoy the show secure in the knowledge that the theatre had been 'disinfected with Jeyes fluid in the interests of public health'.

Though the Olympia had been fitted with a projection box and cinema equipment when it was built in 1911 it was a little ironic that John Maxwell's Scottish Cinema and Variety Theatres, who bought it in 1924, abandoned variety programmes. Ideal as a theatre, the auditorium was not so good as a cinema since many of the seats gave an angled or even an almost side-on view of the screen. In 1938 ABC (of which SCVT had now become part) reconstructed the interior to a design by McNair. The music hall features were lost and a 1,689 seat cinema emerged. Continuous lighting coves flowed from the sleek side walls around the top of the proscenium which was flanked by decorative grilles in striking contrast to the Edwardian exterior. Business was revitalised by the transformation; but not indefinitely. In 1962 the Olympia took the **ABC** name, which seemed as incongruous as the three plastic lozenges forming the name sign on the grand facade. By 1974 the Bridgeton ABC was closed and lay empty for over a decade

152

before becoming a bingo club. Its landmark exterior now has a grade B listing.

The Strathclyde in Summerfield Road, Dalmarnock was advertised as a super cinema but didn't quite live up to the name. Opened in 1928, it was a large, plain structure with a lofty, unadorned auditorium and a wide horseshoe-shaped balcony. A former usherette remembers that it was also a fairly rough house:

> After the war, the Greens rarely got the big hits so there was seldom anything much worth looking at on the screen in there. We got a lot of drunks and they just fell asleep in the warmth of the stalls. Sometimes they would lie full length in the aisles. Well, they would start snoring or, worse, wet themselves. We knew who to throw out because you could see a wee river running down from the culprit and shining silvery in the light from the screen. They could get really nasty if woken up, all fists and swearing at the top of their voices. Thank goodness the ones in the balcony were quite different. They went for the films and were nice old folk, couples mostly. We never had any real trouble up there.

The Strathclyde went on attracting cinema audiences until Mecca bought it for bingo in 1961. It was demolished in 1980 and a pub now occupies the site.

In Bridgeton, certain films were seen as a test of character. Cinema goers had to have strong nerves and prove it. Jimmy Melvin recalls going to the pictures at the Strathclyde in the fifties:

> When we were over eighteen we took our girlfriends to see horror films starring Lon Chaney, who made a great Frankenstein-type actor. These were some of the first pictures to attract an 'H' certificate but they were tame stuff compared with today's productions. Nobody in the audience made a sound. In Brigton, if you screamed you were either 'feart' or 'saft'.

The **Dalmarnock Picture House** in Nuneaton Street was the first in the district to show talking pictures, proudly presenting *The Singing Fool*, starring Al Jolson, in November 1929. This may be the reason it came to be known locally as the 'Geggie', a Glasgow word for mouth! The Dalmarnock, which was renamed the **Plaza** after the Second World War, was very austere inside but fairly grand on the outside with a neo-classical show-facade designed around four pilasters supporting a shallow frieze and pediment. It closed in 1959 to become a warehouse and was demolished in 1981.

The Arcadia, Bridgeton. (Tony Moss)

The **Arcadia** at the corner of Canning Street and London Road was designed by William Beresford Inglis and opened on Hogmanay 1930. Developed in the period between Inglis's superb Boulevard at Knightswood and his even more exotic Toledo at Muirend, the Arcadia displayed very little of their decorative style. The symmetrical, twin-towered frontage on a red sandstone base was formally similar to the Boulevard's but the Arcadia was plain outside and in. Before construction was complete it was bought by ABC and so from the start had some of the best programmes in the area. Unfortunately, it attracted some thuggish audiences. Mrs Cairey always sat in the balcony in case there was trouble:

> In the darkness you could hear a rammy breaking out in the front stalls. People sitting round about you would chant and stamp their feet, and you'd hear FIGHT! (clap, clap, clap)

154

FIGHT! (Clap, clap, clap). Every ruffian in the audience would climb over the seats to watch. They'd pick other fights and all hell would break loose. Then the lights would come on and the ushers would throw the troublemakers out.

In 1939 Harry Winocour bought the Arcadia from ABC but, like other minor exhibitors, he found it difficult to make a profit. In the post-war years competition was stiff and the Entertainment Tax hit low-price picture houses hard. In August 1953, the Arcadia was closed after part of its ceiling collapsed. Building materials were scarce and, besides, there was no money for repairs. Winacour sold out to the Greens in 1954, benefitting both parties; the former made good financially while the latter gained extra circuit strength and, thereby, influence over film renters. The Greens speedily repaired and reopened the Arcadia. In 1962 it passed to Mecca for bingo and in 1971 re-development schemes removed it along with some fine London Road tenements.

> Violence was not uncommon in Bridgeton cinemas. An incident in the Dalmarnock in 1928 led to a brawl in which a girl was struck. Gang law demanded vengeance, and previously friendly gangs met to fight the notorious battle of Albert Bridge. By the mid-thirties, however, the police, reorganised under Chief Constable Percy Sillitoe (later Sir Percy, head of MI5) were bringing things under control. Their secret weapon was a huge policeman, Sergeant Morrison by name, better known to his victims as 'Big Tommy fae the Toll'. Big Tommy was well known around the East End cinemas and stood no nonsense from the gangs, or anyone else.

Opened in 1932, the gigantic, elaborately-designed **Orient** delivered a knockout blow to a number of its smaller rivals. The Orient was a spectacular architectural confection but, even when new, Albert Gardner's last cinema design seemed a little old-fashioned and stylistically haphazard. The eye-catching entrance on the corner of Gallowgate and Sword Street, with its exotic, geometric art deco motifs and unique ziggurat tower, looked modern but lacked a sense of harmony and proportion. The foyer and vestibule were capacious and dominated by a crude stylised sculpture of an amazon on a plinth set into the circle staircase. Elaborately decorated, brightly painted cornices and pilasters gave a foretaste of the spectacular 'atmospheric' treatment within. A warren of dark passages, waiting areas, ante-rooms and stairwells had to be negotiated before emerging into the

The facade of the Orient resembled a giant birthday cake. (Ian Cunningham)

ponderous 2,500 seat auditorium with its large, horseshoe-shaped balcony. In the distance across a sea of seats, the proscenium was formed by an arched bridge in plaster resembling rough-hewn stonework and painted overall in gold, beneath which the screen curtain depicted a landscape with a castle on a hill. On either side Gardner had produced cute Spanish and Norman fantasylands with gates and turrets all made of stucco and lit from within. Customers from the drab Gallowgate agreed it was 'jist luvely'.

The Orient offered excellent value for money; the doors opened at 6.30pm every night and audiences could see a double feature, recent newsreels, cartoons and a documentary before it closed at 11pm – all for 5d! A regular customer remembers that:

> During the thirties the Orient was very busy, though it rarely got films on their first release. Months after they had toured the suburbs, big epics like *The Prisoner of Zenda* would be shown. Sometimes the prints were a bit worn and flickery but the place would be filled to the last seat. These were hard, cramped and squeaky. The Orient was never in the luxury class but, by Jove, it had tremendous atmosphere.

156

Unfortunately, atmospheric cinemas soon showed their weaknesses and, by the fifties, hard use by tough customers had left the flimsily decorated interior very scruffy. It was sold in 1959 by the George Taylor circuit, whose flagship it had been, to the Greens and subsequently to Mecca for bingo. Mecca truncated the facade and renovated the interior in 1985, leaving the Orient gaudier than ever. Declining numbers at the bingo made it difficult to keep up the maintenance and the Orient had become very dilapidated once more before it closed in August 1995. It remains derelict.

The Orient's vast auditorium when new.

Dennistoun

From the 1860s onwards the small estates of rural Dennistoun were developed into a garden suburb of the growing city but, as its population grew, the original detached villas gave way to terraced houses which were in turn replaced by tenements. Despite the district's social decline its inhabitants have always felt a strong local pride; asked where they came from they would usually say Dennistoun rather than Glasgow. Around the time of the First World War, Dennistoun folk considered going into Glasgow a special excursion, tending to find their amusements locally. They flocked to the Dennistoun Palais, one of the biggest dance halls in the Glasgow area, and they were keen picture goers.

In August 1910, James Welsh and George Smith gave their first picture show in the former Parade Roller Skating Rink, up a tenement close on Alexandra Parade. It was soon converted into a 350 seat cinema and renamed the **Alexandra Parade Picture Palace**. The bill for the opening week featured 'Selig's Great Wild West Picture – The Range Riders, Pathé's Beautiful Coloured Pictures, Glimpses of Bird Life' and a local attraction, a 'Special Picture of Lanark Flying Week' (the international aviation meeting had taken place recently). There was also a variety turn, a 'chic comedienne and dancer'. Two performances were given each night at 7pm and 9pm and admission was 2d and 4d. Parents were urged to send their children to the Saturday matinee at which a gift of sweets would be given to each child. Smith and Welsh were so encouraged by their early success that, in the twenties, they moved into a purpose built cinema.

The pioneering exhibitor, Ralph Pringle, also brought film shows to a former skating venue, the Dennistoun Roller Skating Rink. This massive brick shed with a vast, curved, corrugated-iron roof was rebuilt by George Boswell, its original architect, into a dance hall (the first Dennistoun Palais) and a 1,200 seat cinema. The latter was opened as **Pringle's Dennistoun Palladium** on 1 January 1912 to a frosty welcome; the heating system didn't work! This immediately closed the Palladium for a week, but was not the worst of its problems. The back-projection system produced a small, poorly focused image which could hardly be seen from the rear seats and the Palladium was soon overtaken by technical developments and stiff competition from newer rivals. It closed in 1921 and the popular and profitable dance hall took over the entire building.

The Palladium's competitors included the **Marne Picture House** in Marne Street which opened in November 1920. Alex Cameron, a devotee of Dennistoun cinemas while growing up in the district in the thirties, remembers:

> The Saturday matinee at the Marne cost 2d, so it had to be a specially good picture for us children to sacrifice that extra penny. The Marne had an unusual dark, stuffy interior. To the right of the seating area there was a standing space with bars to lean on while waiting to be seated by an usher. This was especially crowded in bad weather. The Marne had such a low ceiling that it could get to be chokingly smoky at times. There was no

balcony, just two areas of more comfortable seats steeply banked on either side of the projection room.

The Marne, whose name had painful First World War connotations, was renamed the **Park Cinema** in 1928 and operated for thirty years before being demolished and replaced by a block of flats.

The Marne had only been in business for three months when Smith and Welsh opened the **Parade** in Meadowpark Street, parallel to Marne Street and just a tenement block away. Unlike its neighbour, the Parade was a robustly built, well finished hall with a lofty auditorium seating over 1,400. There were separate entrances for the stalls and balcony and the seating ranged from leather upholstered benches in the front stalls, costing just 1d and usually crammed with children, through leather tip-ups at the rear, where the courting couples canoodled, to the plush seats in the balcony which attracted the better-off, usually older, customers. The Parade offered good value, with a double feature, a cartoon and newsreels at each performance. But woe betide any customer who lost their ticket stub; these were checked at regular intervals and anyone caught without one was escorted out. With the audience puffing at their pipes and cigarettes (Alex Cameron,

Cinema second time around: the New Parade in the 1970s. (Ian Cunningham)

who was a regular at the Parade as well as the Marne, always thought they looked as though they were quietly cooking with all the smoke rising around them) the hall soon filled with a thick fug and the usherettes spent a lot of time spraying Cromessol, a Glasgow-produced air freshener, around the place.

Smith and Welsh sold the Parade to a Gaumont subsidiary in 1928 and in August 1961 it became the Dennistoun Top Rank Club. But, incredibly, it became a picture house again when Jack Brown, an independent dance hall owner, bought it and opened it as a family cinema, the **New Parade**, in June 1969. The management announced, 'we feel that the family should be catered for and we will never show an X-rated film in this hall. You can't let parents take their children with them to an X-rated film, so we'll put on wholesome entertainment'. Films like *Goldfinger, The Great Escape, The Magnificent Seven* and *Peter Pan* made the New Parade a success initially; remarkable considering the competition from the Granada in Parkhead and the Rex in Riddrie (described below). But by the seventies the old cinema with its ample waiting areas and big balcony was something of an anachronism and needed major refurbishment which the bargain admission

The Dennistoun Picture House. (Tony Moss)

160

prices did not bring in enough money to pay for. It closed when Jack Brown retired in April 1986 and lay derelict until 1993 when the front part was converted into a pub with the facade restored and partially clad in bronze-coloured, reflective glass panels.

The **Dennistoun Picture House**, on the corner of Armadale Street and Findlay Drive, also opened in 1921. Built for independent owners, like so many other speculative cinemas it was absorbed, in 1929, by John Maxwell's Scottish Cinema and Variety Theatres. The rather old-fashioned Picture House had a small tiled frontage and a long narrow entrance hall (divided down the middle into two 'tunnels' to keep the stalls and circles queues separate) leading to a plain, well-kept, 1,373 seat auditorium. For many years its appreciative, mainly older audience enjoyed quality programmes, and epics, such as *The Ten Commandments*, were particularly popular. After forty years of use the Picture House had hardly changed when it was closed for demolition in November 1960.

Riddrie

Riddrie is a sprawling housing scheme with two storey, semi-detached houses stretching as far as the eye can see. It was one of several such schemes developed in the early thirties under the direction of George Smith, Corporation Housing Convenor extraordinaire and director of cinema companies.

In Riddrie, ABC got in before Smith and Welsh when, in December 1931, they opened the **Rex**, a trend-setting, suburban super designed by Charles McNair, on Cumbernauld Road. The exterior of the Rex was very striking. Up to door top level the frontage was clad in faience tiles and a tall, squarely symmetrical facade slit by slim windows soared above a massive canopy. There were extensive waiting rooms with terrazzo floors and rattan couches and a particularly sumptuous auditorium whose quaintly pilastered anteproscenium (the neo-classical overtones of which were slightly out of keeping with the forward-looking exterior design) led the eye to screen curtains decorated with colourful butterflies. The Rex's modern, angular appearance set it apart from previous, rather utilitarian SCVT/ABC cinemas in Glasgow and it became a prototype for ABC's suburban cinemas throughout Britain. As John Maxwell told the audience at the opening, it also 'effected a much needed improvement to the sparse amenities' of its own area, and it was a great success. According to Alex Cameron:

The Rex as the ABC in the 1960s. (Scottish Film Archive)

The Rex was a revelation when it opened. It had upholstered seats . . . thick carpets . . . and hidden lighting, luxuries we had never experienced before. Although its films were a week older than at ABC's Dennistoun Picture House, many people preferred its modern interiors and bigger screen. It was in the Rex in 1939 that I saw the Pathé News about the impending world war. Even at the age of twelve I think I realised the anxiety caused by a possible conflict. Two weeks later I became an evacuee.

Though cinema attendances were never higher than during the war little maintenance was possible and by the fifties the upmarket image of the Rex was tarnished. The decor became tatty and threadbare carpets had to be removed but were not replaced. To make matters worse a small group of thuggish customers made life difficult for the management. One former controller remarked, 'perhaps it was no coincidence that the notorious Barlinnie Prison was only a short walk

162

away'. X-rated films lured young delinquents and many older customers now preferred watching television at home to risking an unpleasantly rowdy night out in increasingly spartan surroundings. In 1961 the Rex was renamed the **ABC** and refurbished to a high standard, but the slump in attendances had already begun and only got worse. Riddrie's ABC closed on 29 September 1973 and was demolished to make way for a car showroom.

It was seven years after the opening of the Rex before George Smith and James Welsh built their own cinema in the area, but the **Riddrie** was worth waiting for. James McKissack's masterpiece still stands on an island site on Cumbernauld Road flaunting more flowing, streamline, moderne curves than any of his other creations. The symmetrical design has a smooth, faience-clad frontage, rising in three finely proportioned stages to the central, fin-shaped, neon name sign, and curving away at various levels to the side walls. Bands of dark amber tiles highlight the front wall up to door level and are carried round the side walls while, from the canopy upwards, each level is trimmed with dark tiling cornices. There was originally a revolving door but, over-

The Riddrie when new in 1938. (Scottish Film Archive)

The foyer of the Riddrie.

enthusiastically used it was prone to damage and was replaced by a secondary pay-box. Inside broad curving stairways led to the lofty, 1,780 seat auditorium where the moderne decor was continued. Most of the ornamentation was concentrated around the proscenium and consisted of ranks of towering round columns flanking the exits. Above the exit doors stylish, illuminated, oblong clock faces were set in decorated recesses. The original colour scheme was a sophisticated silver, cream and two tones of blue and the silver proscenium arch was suffused in complementary blue, green and red holphane light.

In January 1950, Smith and Welsh sold the Riddrie to George Singleton who ran it much as before, though he changed the name to his standard, **Vogue**, which was particularly apt for the sleek, glamorous building. Television caught on quickly in residential areas such as Riddrie and the Vogue and the Rex both suffered. The Rex cultivated audience support through its children's club and benefitted from the commercial strength of a national circuit, but the Vogue had neither of these advantages. The Singletons realised that whichever went over to bingo first was most likely to survive and the Vogue became a bingo hall in 1968, a move which saved the exceptional building from destruction. A hideous mustard, red and purple colour scheme was introduced but otherwise the former picture house has been well looked after. In May 1989, the Vogue became a film star when it was floodlit to act the part of a super cinema in *The Big Man*,

*Interior of the Vogue
as a bingo club.
(Scott McCutcheon)*

a film about the exploits of a bare knuckle fighter, set in the fifties and starring Liam Neeson. In 1994, Ronald Singleton, the third generation representative of the cinema-owning family, retired and his properties were taken over by a new company, Jaro Ltd. Further renovation of the Vogue seems inevitable. It still serves its customers well and is the most completely preserved example of a streamline, art deco cinema building in Glasgow.

Parkhead

Two cinemas opened in 1909 at the Parkhead end of the Gallowgate. **Scott's Annfield Electric Theatre** took over the former Annfield Halls and the **Empire Electric Picture Palace** opened at number 1281. The Empire Electric closed in 1925 but, surprisingly, Scott's lasted until 1934.

The **Louvre** was one of a number of picture houses to be built around Parkhead Cross. Opened in 1914, just a little way along Duke Street from the Cross, its twin-towered facade fronted a long, narrow, 955 seat hall which was acquired in 1934 by Bernard Frutin and demolished to make way for the Granada (see below).

During its uneventful career the Louvre's closest competitor was the **Parkhead Picture Palace**, opened in August 1921 at 49 Tollcross Road, another of the streets radiating out from the Cross. 'The Three P's', as it was known, was initially an upmarket cinema. Its angular tiled entrance portico was set into a two-storey tenement and a long tunnel led to the foyer and the 1,250 seat auditorium in which there was a small balcony, arcaded aisles and Corinthian columns along the side walls supporting a barrel-vaulted ceiling. The Three P's was always reliably profitable, even in the thirties when business declined in the face of tough, super cinema competition and the hall became anything but palatial. Latterly, it came to be regarded as an unworthy stable-mate for the other SCVT/ABC cinemas and was never mentioned in group advertising. According to a former projectionist, 'The Three P's became a real dump as the years went by and there was cut-throat competition between it and Green's Picturedrome (in Tollcross). Kids were bribed into one with balloons and into the other with a consignment of old comics'. The children's business was important to struggling cinemas and managers didn't worry too much about the rating laws in letting them in. Gordon Coombes, an ABC circuit controller, recalls a visit he paid to the Parkhead Picture Palace one afternoon during the school holidays. He found the cinema packed with youngsters of all ages apparently thoroughly enjoying *Detective Story*. 'This film, starring Kirk Douglas, William Bendix and Eleanor Parker, was one of the first to be X-rated when the category was introduced in

The eyecatching frontage of the Granada shortly after becoming a bingo club. (Ian Cunningham)

1951. Horrified, I confronted the manager only to receive his airy assurance,"Och, naebody takes ony notice of certificates in here!" '
The Three P's was destroyed by a fire in August 1960.

The mighty **Granada** brought unprecedented cinema grandeur to industrial Parkhead. Opened on 26 August 1934 by Sir Charles Clelland, then acting chairman of the British Film Institute, it was a *tour de force* of jazz-moderne styling. Though modest in size, the brilliantly white portico (painted twice a year to ensure it remained dazzling) on Duke Street was impressive. Above the wide doorway and canopy rose a tower with vertical ribs and a pediment (inspired by New York's skyscrapers), flanked by sweeping stucco-clad panels carrying advertising hoardings announcing the latest programmes. At night it was floodlit and banded in red and green neon, a glittering echo of the Empire State Building or Miami Beach. Among the smoke-blackened tenements facing the belching chimneys and corrugated iron mass of Beardmore's Parkhead Forge it must have been very seductive.

Once through the vestibule, clutching a ticket bought at either the circle or the stalls pay-box, customers made their way to the lofty double-level foyer where tall, fluted pilasters on the walls burst into a riot of waves and zig-zags at ceiling height. A wide staircase with travertine balustrades, straight out of a musical spectacular, led to the splendid balcony. In the auditorium, the proscenium was formed by bands of green, blue and purple plaster waves flowing out towards

The vast auditorium of the Granada as a bingo hall.

ceiling and walls, the speaker grilles represented skyscrapers with towers and spires in low relief plasterwork, and red and black dado panels lined the side walls underlining murals of Spanish scenes, the only allusion to the Granada's name. There were private boxes on either side of the projection room which, unusually, was located below the circle, and comfortable, high-backed theatre seats throughout.

Shortly after it opened, the Granada was plunged into controversy when Sidney Bernstein, who owned a chain of lavish Granada cinemas in London suburbs, objected to the Frutins using what he regarded as his trade name. His attempt to get a court order against them was rejected; Bernstein's nearest cinema was three hundred miles away in Bedford! The Parkhead Granada settled down to a successful and highly profitable career as the Frutin's busiest picture house. The ample stage facilities were occasionally used for variety turns until the fifties and the Granada remained luxurious and busy throughout the sixties' slump, presenting revivals of good films first shown at city centre cinemas. Nevertheless it closed on 13 June 1971 with *Best of the Badmen*, starring Robert Ryan, and *Men of Sherwood Forest*, and Mecca converted it into a bingo hall. The facade had to be cut down because of water damage to the stucco work and it is now clad in ugly grey sheet metal but, although the murals have gone, the splendid interior remains substantially intact. It was closed in 1995 when a new bingo club opened in the second phase of the Forge shopping centre development.

In April 1989, Cannon opened a seven-screen multiplex cinema in the shopping centre which now occupies the site of the mighty Parkhead Forge. The **Cannon Parkhead Forge**, the first custom-built picture house to open in Glasgow since the ABC 2, was designed by Howard and Unick who became the acknowledged leader in multiplex design. The eye-catching pyramid-shaped aluminium and glass exterior (shared with the shopping centre) houses a cluster of superbly appointed auditoria with near perfect sightlines. There are disabled access facilities and even shower rooms for the staff. The singer Lulu performed the opening ceremony (but didn't stay to see the first film) as part of a spectacular send-off involving marching bands, a fair in the car park and a special appearance of the motor car from *Chitty Chitty Bang Bang*. In September 1992 it became the first cinema in Scotland to assume the name **MGM**. Although it lacks the sense of occasion created by some of the cinemas of the 'Golden Age' it has been a major boost to Glasgow's entertainment facilities and its great success is the most tangible sign of a renaissance in the city's cinema business.

168

Shettleston and Tollcross

In its spread eastwards Glasgow engulfed a number of villages and traces of village mentality were long to be found in the East End. The natives of such districts as Shettleston and Tollcross, for instance, were quite peeved if outsiders mixed the two up. The inhabitants of Shettleston in particular felt a strong sense of community stemming from long before its farms and weavers' cottages were swamped by industrial works and streets of tenements. But, having become sub-urbs, Tollcross and Shettleston gradually merged so that nowadays it is difficult to see where the boundary between them lies. Tollcross Park, their boundary with Parkhead, is clearer but all three areas have a lot in common, including their fondness for the movies.

Though several of the big players set up business in Shettleston, George Urie Scott dominated the district's cinema scene from start to finish. He opened the area's first two cinemas in 1912. The Shettleston **Scott's Electric Theatre** was fashioned out of the Parkhead Wire Works, a flat-floored, brick shed which he packed with wooden benches and kept open until 1920. **The Premier**, in Shettleston Road, was a back-court conversion, reached through a shop, in which Scott began penny matinees during the First World War. It lasted until 1948 and can still be identified in the Irish social club known as 'The Barn'.

The Palaceum after its 1936 rebuild.

Another Scott-controlled cinema, the grandly-named **Palaceum**, in Edrom Street, brought the refinement of upholstered, tip-up seats to the district in 1913. It was a fine, small picture house with a handsomely theatrical, rendered brick frontage with pavilionate towers at either end. In the thirties, although its films were a week older than at the newer super cinemas, the Palaceum was cheaper to visit and had the added attraction of variety acts which, though unpolished, were considered by local folk, especially the older ones, to add to the entertainment and the value for money of the show. In 1936, Scott had the Palaceum rebuilt. The new entrance portico was plain, square and very functional, with a fin-shaped name sign and a huge hoarding dominating the facade, and the interior decoration was completely modernised. These changes no doubt helped the Palaceum hold its own until, after a fire, it was demolished in 1954.

George Green opened a **Picturedrome** in Wellshot Road in 1914. It had a simple, roughcast frontage detailed in red sandstone with separate front and rear stalls entrances either side of a bay window and a plain, long, rectangular hall. Like the other Picturedromes it became famous for its Tom Mix and Pearl White cowboy serials and its penny matinees. Adults tended to avoid the Picturedrome. Those brave enough to venture there were usually chaperoning smaller children unable to look after themselves in the survival of the fittest. When the Wild West adventures ceased to entertain the children, they amused themselves by spitting up into the projector beam or pulling lumps of stuffing out of the seats to throw at each other. The Picturedrome came to be known as 'The Scum'.

The young George Singleton also wanted a piece of the cinema action in this populous working class district and it was here that, aged 29, he embarked on his first completely new, purpose built cinema project. He consulted Smith and Welsh about finance and policy and it was through them that his long collaboration with James McKissack, who was to design all Singleton's impressive suburban cinemas, began with the Shettleston **Broadway**. George Singleton takes up the story:

> We found a site just off Shettleston Road. It was cramped and on an awkward corner and James McKissack was asked to make a very conspicuous entranceway that could be seen from Shettleston Road. It didn't matter what it looked like as long as it was eye-catching and everyone could see that it was there. He did us proud. James Welsh chose the name to match up with his other halls and it had the right Hollywood feel. I was very proud

of the Broadway. It was my first big achievement when I went into the cinema trade and it cost £30,000; not much in today's terms maybe, but a great deal then.

The Broadway was indeed dominated by the prominent entranceway ordered by its owners; a monumental corner portico almost three storeys high, clad in creamy gold tiling and embellished with Egypto-Greek motifs. To save on land acquisition costs the rest of a lofty hall was compactly built, with a two-level foyer whose enormous windows, lit from inside, made an inviting advertisement for the cinema. The plush, 1,700 seat auditorium, painted in red and turquoise with crimson and green zig-zag patterned carpets and pale green screen curtains bordered with sunflowers, brought a new level of cinema luxury to Shettleston. George Urie Scott was not amused, and was more dismayed when the Broadway was sold to Odeon in September 1936, giving the giant English circuit a foothold in Glasgow and the rival cinema access to the best recent films. The **Odeon** was to give Scott a run for his money until 1967 when it bowed out of films and became a Mecca bingo hall for several years before being demolished.

Faced with the Broadway's competitive advantages after its transformation into the Odeon, Scott needed to take drastic action. In July 1936, he applied for planning permission for what would be Shettleston's biggest and grandest cinema. The **State**, on Shettleston Road, was designed by Charles McNair and built by Scott's own Cinema Construction Company. Local schoolchildren were given conducted tours of the new wonder cinema even before it opened and the grand opening was on 14 May 1937. Billy Carlisle and Phyllis Tremaine, the stars of the famous *Half Past Eight Show* gave an impromptu stage performance and William Powell and Jean Harlow starred in *Libelled Lady* before a large audience, which included many East End cinema owners and managers eager to see what Scott was up to.

Scott proudly described the State as 'modern architecture at its restrained best' and the tall, brilliant-white, vertically-ribbed facade, split by a massive red name sign and outlined at night in blue, green and red neon was glitzy, gleaming and self-confident. The interior was even more remarkable. Splendid hallways with coloured terrazzo floors, streamlined chromium balustrades and gorgeous multicoloured cove lighting were furnished with moderne-style rattan couches and elegant column ashtrays. The 2,000 seat auditorium was especially attractive and was advertised as 'air conditioned to make cinema going a physical as well as a mental pleasure'. The publicity even announced the toilets as of 'an exceptional standard for a neighbourhood cinema'.

171

The relatively high admission prices, from 4d in the front stalls to a shilling in the circle, reflected the superior appointments.

The State had a long, untroubled career as one of the East End's top picture houses, always maintaining the traditions of a family cinema. Even late in its career the manager would appear in evening dress to bid patrons good night. But, by the sixties, good quality family films became harder to find and the imposition of VAT on cinema admissions in 1972 was bad for business. The State closed for a fortnight in protest, but to no avail. In February 1973, the management booked *Song of Norway*, a musical based on the life of Edvard Greig, which was a great flop in Shettleston, taking only £77 in its first three days. It was hastily replaced for the rest of the week, but the writing was on the wall. Ironically, the State's last film, *Enter the Dragon* with Bruce Lee, was a resounding success, taking over £1,000. On 4 May 1973, a full house bade farewell to this fine cinema. Thirteen years of dereliction followed during which the proud, red name sign was removed and peeling paint, broken windows and slapped-on advertising billboards made the empty building an eyesore. It was demolished in July 1986 and a Halford's store now occupies the site.

The State in August 1937. (Strathclyde Regional Archives)

Glossary

Architrave	moulding round an arch or door frame.
'Atmospheric'	style of cinema decoration in which artificial three dimensional buildings and scenery recreate an exotic location.
Balustrade	vertical supports of stair handrail.
Bas-relief	sculpture in low relief.
Cartouche	ornament, usually plaster, consisting of tablet surrounded by scrolls.
CinemaScope	wide screen format (aspect ratio 2.55:1) introduced in 1953.
Corbel	stone projection from a wall to support weight.
Coving	protrusion, usually at ceiling height, often used to conceal lighting.
Crush hall	indoor area for waiting or forming queues.
Faience	coloured earthenware tiles or mouldings.
Ferrule	short cylindrical ornament.
Holophane	specialist lighting company which produced effects lighting commonly used in cinemas.
Jazz-moderne	1930s style using bright colours, etched glass, zig-zags, wave patterns and stylised sunbursts.
Loggia	a covered open arcade or balcony fronted by columns.
Moderne	1930s style using parallel lines, curves, fin-shaped signage, and tall, narrow windows; also known as streamline moderne.
Mullion	vertical bar dividing a window or separating windows.
Ogee	S-shaped moulding.
Nickelodeon	small, primitive cinema with single level of seating.
Pediment	low pitched gable over an entrance or facade.

Pilaster	rectangular column projecting slightly from a **wall**.
Portico	entrance porch.
Proscenium	the opening around the stage or screen.
Repertory	film exhibition policy whereby old films are reprised for short periods.
Roadshow	film exhibition policy whereby recent films are initially released only at selected circuit cinemas.
Slip	narrow extension of balcony along sidewall.
Splay walls	angled side walls of auditorium.
Stadium-plan	auditorium with one level of raked seating.
Steppings	seating terraces on cinema balcony.
Streamline	moderne (see Moderne).
Swags	moulded plaster representations of drapes.
Terrazzo	patterns of marble or other chips set in concrete and polished to form an ornate floor.
Travertine	white or light-coloured marble often used to colour terrazzo.

Gazeteer

Name of building when first opened as cinema; street; district; o=date opened; name of owner/operator; a=architect; s=seating capacity; alterations and fate; c=closure date; cd=closed and demolished shortly after; d=demolished after a spell of dereliction or subsequent use.

ABC 2 298 Sauchiehall Street; City Centre; o 19.10.67 by ABC; a Leslie C. Norton and C.J. Foster; s 922; became screen 2 in 5-screen MGM Cinemas.

ALDWYCH 2130 Paisley Road West; Cardonald; o 16.4.38 by George Smith and James Welsh; a James McKissack; s 2,500; sold to Singleton Cinemas Ltd 7.1.50; c 1963; bingo; d 1964; supermarket.

ARCADIA 484 London Road; Bridgeton; o 31.12.30 by ABC; a William Beresford Inglis; s 1,409; sold to Harry Winocour 1939; sold to George Green Ltd 15.11.54; c 2.4.62; bingo; d 1971.

ARDGOWAN 177 Wier Street; Tradeston; o 1923 by James Hamilton; a Eric A. Sutherland; s 1,116; c 1963; d 1965.

ARGYLE ELECTRIC THEATRE Argyle Street; City Centre; o 23.12.10 by Argyle Pictures and Varieties; a George A. Boswell; s 754; rebuilt and reopened 21.11.38 by Argyle Picture House Ltd; a Boswell; s 1,250; c 21.3.60; d 1963; Argyle St train station.

ASCOT 1544 Great Western Road; Anniesland; o 6.12.39 by Great Western Cinemas; a Charles J. McNair and Elder; s 1,963; sold to Gaumont 2.43 and renamed Gaumont 7.50; renamed Odeon 5.64; c 25.10.75; bingo from 1979; listed building.

ASTORIA 67 Possil Road; Possil; o 2.2.31 by Astoria Cinema Ltd; a Albert V. Gardner; s 3,002; sold to CMA (Rank) 23.4.55; c 19.11.62; bingo; d 1995.

AVENUE 950 Dumbarton Road; Whiteinch; o 5.2.13 by Scotstoun

Pictures and Varieties Ltd; a Thomas Baird Jnr; s 700; sold to James Graham 1919; rebuilt and reopened 5.6.30 as the Victoria; a Lennox and McMath; sold to Associated G.P. Cinemas 4.4.45; renamed Victory Theatre; rebuilt 1949; a Lennox D. Paterson; sold to Loray Cinema Circuit 5.56; c 1964; warehouse; d 1981.

B.B. CINERAMA Victoria Road/Cutherbetson St; Eglinton Toll; o 14.9.12 by J.J. Bennell; a J. Campbell Reid; s 1,500; cd 1922.

B.B. CINERAMA 201 Victoria Road/Butterbiggins Road; Eglinton Toll; o 1922 by J.J. Bennell; a McInnes Gardner and J. Campbell Reid; s 2,004; sold to Gaumont 1929; rebuilt 1931; a James L. Ross; s 2,662; renamed New Cinerama 1948; rebuilt 1964 and renamed Odeon; s 2,003; c 6.10.81; d 1986; filling station.

BLACK CAT 830 Springfield Road; Bridgeton; o 1921 by A.E. Pickard; a George A. Boswell; s 893; sold 2.45 to Springfield Entertainments Ltd; c 9.55; BBC TV studio and rehearsal rooms; warehouse from 1970.

BLYTHSWOOD 218 Maryhill Road; Maryhill; o 19.12.27 by Blythswood Picture House Ltd; a Charles J. McNair; s 1,100; c 10.8.72; bingo; d 1980; flats.

BOULEVARD 2 Knightscliffe Avenue, Knightswood; o 10.12.28 by North British Theatres Ltd; a William Beresford Inglis; s 1,140; sold 3.11.38 to Singleton Cinemas Ltd; rebuilt; a Inglis; s 1,470; c 1.6.59; d 1960; B&Q car park.

BRIDGETON CROSS ELECTRIC THEATRE 2-28 Olympia Street; Bridgeton; o 1910 by West of Scotland Electric Theatres; a George A. Boswell; leased to George Green Ltd from 1912 and renamed Greens' Picturedrome; cd 1932.

BROADWAY 19 Amulree Street; Shettleston; o 25.6.30 by Singleton Cinemas Ltd; a James McKissack; s 1,742; sold to Odeon 9.36 and renamed Odeon; c 25.1.67; bingo; d 8.95.

CALDER 302 Calder Street; Govanhill; o 25.4.32 by Harry Winocour; a Cowiesons (builders); s 1,250; sold to George Green Ltd 1954; c 1967; bingo until 1972; d 1981; play area.

CAMBRIDGE 90 New City Road; Cowcaddens; o. 8.11.22 by Grove Picture House Ltd; a J. Jeffrey Waddell; s 895; rebuilt 1927; a Charles J. McNair; s 1,020; renovated 3.54; s 954; cd 1964.

CAMPHILL PICTURE HOUSE 7 Baker Street; Shawlands; o 1911 by James Hamilton; a Thomas Baird Jnr; s 820; sold to ABC 8.29. s 1,200; destroyed by fire 22.4.31; d.

CANADIAN PICTURE HOUSE 319 Springburn Road; Springburn; o 1912 by Mary Byatt; a Charles J. McNair; s 440; rebuilt 1921; a McNair, c 10.25; d.

CANNON CINEMAS Forge Shopping Centre; Parkhead; o 28.4.89 by Cannon Cinemas; a Howard and Unick; s 434, 434, 322, 260, 208, 144, 132; renamed MGM Cinemas 11.9.92.

CAPITOL Lorne St; Ibrox; o 11.4.27 by Harry Kemp; a John Fairweather; s 2,062; sold to Gaumont 1928; renamed Gaumont 1954; c 5.8.61; bingo.

CARLTON 150 Castle St; Townhead; o 4.1.26 by James Graham; a Duff and Cairns; s 1,619; sold to Glasgow and West of Scotland Theatres 4.4.45; sold to CMA (Rank) 23.4.55; cd 5.3.66.

CASINO 149/155 Castle Street; Townhead; o 23.10.11 by A.E. Pickard; a George A. Boswell; s 987; sold to Glasgow Casino Ltd 3.24; c 17.2.65; bingo until 1968; d 1973.

CASINO Shawbridge St; Pollockshaws; o 1911 by P. McKenna; s 300; cd 1915.

CATHCART PICTURE HOUSE 15 Old Castle Road; Cathcart; o 1913 by Cathcart Cinemas Ltd; a Charles J. McNair; s 800; rebuilt and re-opened 5.11.28.a McNair; s 1,311; renamed Rialto; sold to ABC 3.30; sold to Associated G.P. Cinemas 1946; renamed George 23.12.48; c 1961; bowling alley; Jehovah's Witness hall from 1969. d 2.94.

CHARING CROSS ELECTRIC THEATRE 508 Sauchiehall Street; City Centre; o 12.5.10 by West of Scotland Electric Theatres; a George A. Boswell; s 454; c 4.26; converted to Locarno Ballroom; Berkeley Casino from 1989.

CINEMA PICTURE HOUSE Renfield St; City Centre; o 25.12.11 by Glasgow Picture House Ltd; a Neil C. Duff; s 633; rebuilt 1920 and renamed Regent; a Duff; s 1,314; damaged by fire 1971; renovated; cd 30.5.82; Regent House (offices).

CITY PICTURE HOUSE 60 Union Street; City Centre; o 28.6.13 by City Picture House Ltd; a William L.E. Aitken; s 400; c 1923; shop.

COMMODORE 1297 Dumbarton Road; Scotstoun; o 1.1.33 by Singleton Cinemas Ltd; a James McKissack; s 2,000; sold to Odeon 9.36 and renamed Odeon; c 25.11.67; d 1976.

COLISEUM 97 Eglinton St; Laurieston; o 18.12.05 by Moss's Empires; a Frank Matcham; s 2,893; sold 2.3.25 to ABC; rebuilt and reopened 7.9.31; a William R. Glen; s 3,094; rebuilt and reopened 26.9.63 as Coliseum Cinerama; a Leslie C. Norton; s 1,310; c 11.10.80. bingo from 1987.

COLOSSEUM Jamaica Street; City Centre; o 30.11.1896 by Walter Wilson; s 500; c 1904; incorporated into Paisley's Store; d 2.94.

CORONATION 470 Cathedral Street; City Centre; o 21.10.11 by Coronation Picture House Ltd; a Duncan and Copland; s 1,000; c 3.12; reopened 9.12 by Central Picture House Ltd; cd 4.15.

COSMO 12 Rose Street; City Centre; o 18.5.39 by Scottish Repertory Cinemas; a James McKissack and W.J. Anderson II; s 850; foyer rebuilt 1964; a Gillespie, Kidd and Coia; rebuilt and reopened 1.5.74 as Glasgow Film Theatre; s 404; screen 2 opened 1988; s 144; listed building.

CRANSTON'S CINEMA DE LUXE 15 Renfield Street; City Centre; o 22.5.16 by Cranston's Pictures Ltd; a James Miller; s 850; sold to Harry Winocour 2.34; sold to George Green Ltd 1954; News Theatre opened adjunct by Capital and Provincial News Theatres 26.7.54; both cinemas sold to Classic 23.9.60; Tatler Cinema Club opened adjoining 4.69; cinema complex renamed Classic Film Centre 5.72; s 644,220,136; destroyed by fire 22.5.81; d 1986; facade restored; Classic House (offices).

CROSSHILL PICTURE HOUSE 488 Victoria Road; Govanhill; o 1920 by J.M. Drummond; a Joseph Boyd; s 650; c 1952; shop.

CROWN 163 Crown Street; Gorbals; o 1914 by J.M. Drummond; a William Reid; s 350; d 1930.

CROWN 163 Crown Street; Gorbals; o 1930 by J.M. Drummond; a Lennox and McMath; s 900; sold to Associated G.P. Cinemas 4.48; Renamed George; c 14.9.70; d 1974.

DALMARNOCK PICTURE HOUSE 361 Nuneaton Street; Bridgeton; o 4.22 by Samuel Gratton; s 1,204; renamed Plaza 8.45; c 8.5.59; warehouse, d 1981.

DENNISTOUN PICTURE HOUSE Armadale Street/Finlay Drive; Dennistoun; o 1921 by Dennistoun Picture House Ltd; a Charles J. McNair; s 1,631; sold to ABC 1929; c 5.11.60. d 1971.

EMBASSY 146 Kilmarnock Road; Shawlands; o 3.2.36 by Harry Winocour; a James McKissack; s 1,638; sold 14.6.38 to Glasgow Photo Playhouse; cd 5.65; supermarket.

EGLINTON ELECTREUM 25 Eglinton St; Laurieston; o 14.12.11

by Eglinton Electreum Ltd; a James McKissack; s 650; cd 5.55.

ELDER Reid Street (Rathlin St); Govan; o 11.12.16 by Caledon Pictures Ltd; a Albert V. Gardner; s 1,121; c 28.3.59; bingo 1967–70; d 6.76.

ELECTRIC PICTURE PALACE 26–30 Maryhill Road; Maryhill; o 8.11.10 by George Urie Scott; a Neil C. Duff; s 600; cd 1950.

ELECTRIC PICTURE PALACE Stonelaw Road; Rutherglen; o 3.2.11 by Rutherglen Electric Theatre Ltd; s 600; c 1930; billiard hall; d c.1968.

EMPIRE Bellahouston Park; o 3.5.38 as part of Empire Exhibition; a Alister G. MacDonald; s 600; cd 29.10.38.

EMPIRE ELECTRIC 106 Napiershall Street; Woodside; o 1910 by P. McKenzie; c 1913.

EMPIRE ELECTRIC PICTURE PALACE 1281 Gallowgate; Parkhead; o 5.10.09 by Empire Picture Palace Ltd; c 1925; working men's club; d 1983.

EMPIRE ERAGRAPH 60 Raglan Street; Woodside; o 1913 by P. McKenzie; c 1931.

EMPRESS THEATRE 313 St George's Road; Woodside; o 4.8.13 as West End Playhouse by Harry McKelvie; a W.B. Whittie; s 1,300; c 2.14; reopened 30.3.14 as Empress Variety and Picture Playhouse by Harry Goodwin; sold to George Urie Scott 4.33; variety theatre with cinema seasons; sold to Falcon Trust 1960; cinema seasons abandoned; renamed Falcon Theatre; sold to Alex Frutin 6.62; renamed New Metropole; sold to Jimmy Logan 5.64; renamed Jimmy Logan's Metropole; c 3.72; d 4.87.

EMPRESS 557 Govan Street (now Ballater St); Gorbals; o 25.11.12 by Empress Pictures Ltd; a James Austen Laird; s 240; c 1914; industrial units.

FLORIDA 162 Ardmay Crescent; King's Park; o 31.12.31 by Florida (Glasgow) Ltd; a Hamilton Neil, revised plans by Lennox and McMath; s 1,640; sold to Gaumont 1938; renamed Gaumont 1949; cd 5.1.57.

GAIETY 625 Argyle Street; Anderston; former Tivoli Theatre of 1898; o 19.12.09 by J.J. Bennell; s 2,000; sold to Anderston Pictures and Varieties Ltd 7.28. Renovated 4.35; a Charles J. McNair; s 1,403; leased to Glasgow Corporation and renamed Glasgow Concert Hall from 29.1.63; cd 31.7.68.

GARRICK 197 Dumbarton Road; Partick; o 22.1.16 by Garrick Cinema Company Ltd; a H. Campbell; s 900; renamed Western Cinema 1919; owners Western Cinema Company Ltd; rebuilt 1921; a Charles J. McNair; s 1,211; c 1966; d 4.79.

GOVAN CINEMA 729 Govan Road; Govan; o 20.6.13 by Scottish Cinema and Variety Theatres; a Richard Hendersons; s 1,209; cd 4.36.

GOVAN CROSS PICTURE PALACE 51–55 Helen Street; Govan; o 5.8.10 by James Hamilton; a James C. Robertson; s 1,282; c 1929; warehouse.

GOVANHILL PICTURE HOUSE 49 Bankhall Street; Govanhill; o 2.5.26 by James Hamilton; a Eric A. Sutherland; s 1,200; sold to ABC 4.11.29; s 1148; c 20.5.61; bingo until 1974; warehouse.

GRAFTON 243 Parliamentary Road; Cowcaddens; o 1922 by Albert Pictures Ltd; a Duff and Cairns; s 1,040; cd 1964.

GRANADA 1321 Duke Street; Parkhead; o 26.8.35 by Bernard Frutin; a Lennox and McMath; s 2,400; c 13.6.72; bingo; c 8.95; derelict.

GRAND CENTRAL 20 Jamaica Street; City Centre; o 9.8.15 by Henry Meiklejohn; a W.B. Whittie; s 750; c 1966; reopened 1973 as Classic Grand by Classic Cinemas; s 365; renamed Cannon 1.85; c 4.5.92; derelict.

GRAND CENTRAL Main Street; Rutherglen; o 17.3.21 by Grand Central (Rutherglen) Ltd; a S. Adams; s 950; cd 20.12.57.

GRANVILLE 164 Great Western Road; Woodside; o 1921 by Granville Picture House Ltd; a George M. Brand; s 550; renovated 1928 and renamed Gem; owners Gem Cinema Ltd; s 592; c 1958; car showroom; d 1981.

GREEN'S PAVILION Stonelaw Road; Rutherglen; o 1914 by George Green Ltd; a John Fairweather; s 920; renovated 4.36 and renamed Green's Cinema; c 3.59; car showroom; d 1985.

GREEN'S PICTUREDROME 21 Govan St (now Ballater St); Gorbals; o 3.11 by George Green Ltd; a Thomas Baird Jnr; s 1,100; c 2.58; d *c.*1966.

GREEN'S PICTUREDROME 41 Possil Road; Possil; o 1912 by George Green Ltd; a Burnet and Boston; s 500; leased to Round Toll Pictures Ltd from 3.20 and renamed Round Toll Cinema; c 9.31; sold to R. Pennycook; reopened 6.4.32 as Magnet; cd 4.5.55.

GREEN'S PICTUREDROME 371 Wellshot Road; Tollcross; o 1914 by George Green Ltd; a John Fairweather; s 1,116; renovated 1926 and renamed the Cinema; a Fairweather; cd 2.58.

GREEN'S PLAYHOUSE 126 Renfield Street; City Centre; o 15.9.27 by George Green Ltd; a John Fairweather with decoration by John Alexander; s 4,368; dance hall, tea rooms and putting range adjoining; c 30.6.73; leased to Unicorn Leisure and reopened 8.9.73 as Apollo; s 3,500; c 16.6.85; ballroom destroyed by fire; d 9.87.

GROSVENOR 194 Byres Road; Hillhead; o 3.5.21 by Glasgow Grovenor Ltd; a Albert V. Gardner and William R. Glen; s 1,337; sold 10.29 to ABC; sold 24.5.76 to CAC; s 1,035; rebuilt and reopened 5.12.80; entrance now on Ashton Lane; s 276, 253.

GROVE 12 Breadalbane Street; Anderston; o 4.8.15 by James Graham; a Albert V. Gardner; s 827; sold 4.22 to P. McNicol; c 18.1.32; dance hall; d.

HAMPDEN PICTURE HOUSE 91 Westmoreland Street; Govanhill; o 4.12.20 by Hampden Picture House Ltd; a John Eadie; s 1,040; sold to George Green Ltd 1956; c 1969; bingo until 1974; cycling club; Clada Social Club from 1976.

HILLHEAD PICTURE SALON 17 Vinicombe Street; Hillhead; o 4.10.13 by Hillhead Picture House Co; a Brand and Lithgow; s 672; rebuilt 1931; a James McKissack; s 544; sold 4.69 to Fyfe and Fyfe Ltd; renovated and reopened 20.4.70; s 406; renamed Salon; sold to CAC 3.88 and renovated; c 12.10.92; derelict; listed building.

HIPPODROME Rutherglen Road; Oatlands; o 5.21 by Archibald Horsley; a William Beresford Inglis; s 1,100; leased to Bernard Frutin from 3.25; sold to ABC 21.9.31; renamed Ritz and rebuilt; a Charles J. McNair; cd 18.2.61.

IBROX CINEMATOGRAPH THEATRE Lendel Place; Ibrox; o 8.10 by A.E. Pickard; a Neil C. Duff; s 1,000; c 5.15; warehouse; d 1986.

IMPERIAL 2–6 Govan Road; Cessnock; o 2.1.21 by Henry Meiklejohn; a William Beresford Inglis; s 1,100; damaged by fire 3.52; rebuilt; c 1959; Grand Ole Opry Social Club.

KELVIN 1073 Argyle St; Finnieston; o 12.5.30 by Kelvin Cinema Ltd; a Albert V. Gardner; s 1,957; sold 7.31 to George Taylor; c 1959; boxing arena; bingo from 22.3.73; nightclub from 1981; derelict from 1986; restaurant from 1992.

THE KINEMA 319 Springburn Road; Springburn; o 3.26 by Percy

Byatt; a Albert V. Gardner; s 850; sold to George Green Ltd 1954; cd 1958.

KING'S PICTURE THEATRE 59 James Street; Bridgeton; o 1910 by Samuel Gratton; s 1,400; frontage rebuilt 1936; c 8.5.59; warehouse.

KINGSWAY 1235 Cathcart Road; Cathcart; o 8.5.29 by Kingsway Cinema Ltd (Smith and Welsh); a James McKissack; s 1,432; sold 7.1.50 to Singleton Cinemas Ltd and renamed Vogue; c 3.65; bingo until 6.86; derelict.

LA SCALA 157 Sauchiehall Street; City Centre; o 17.10.12 by Glasgow Photo Playhouse Ltd; a Neil C. Duff and James McKissack; s 1,000; rebuilt 8.36; a Alister G. MacDonald; s 1,300; twinned 8.4.76; café converted to third screen 6.3.78; s 650, 250, 110; renamed Scalas 23.1.81; c 28.5.84; Mark One shop.

LONDON ROAD PICTURE PALACE Kirkpatrick Street; Bridgeton; o 1910 by J.J. Bennell; a Purdie and Gillespie; s 700; sold to R.V. Singleton 6.27; J.T. Singleton from 1940; c 9.57; warehouse.

LORNE Cornwall Street; Ibrox; o 11.1.14 by Lorne Cinema House Ltd; a Neil C. Duff; s 900; sold to Caledon Pictures Ltd and rebuilt 3.28. a Albert V. Gardner; s 1,265; c 1968; bingo until 1976; d 1982.

LOUVRE 1313–24 Duke Street; Parkhead; o 1914 by Parkhead X Picture House Ltd; a Halley and Neil; s 955; cd 1934.

LYCEUM 908 Govan Road; Govan; o 4.11.99 as Lyceum Theatre; film shows from 1902; sold to Caledon Pictures Ltd 11.23; s 3,000; rebuilt 1932; a Charles J. McNair; s 2,078; destroyed by fire 24.10.37.

LYCEUM 908 Govan Road; Govan; o 19.12.38 by Caledon Pictures Ltd; a Charles J. McNair and Elder; s 2,600; sold 27.7.74 to County Properties and Developments Ltd; reopened 25.11.74; s 480; c 12.1.81; bingo.

LYRIC 100 Langlands Road; Govan; o 9.10.22 by Bernard Frutin; a Charles J. McNair; s 645; c 3.33; converted to La Marina Ballroom; d 1982.

LYRIC THEATRE 60 Sauchiehall Street; City Centre; built 1879 as Royalty Theatre; a Frank Matcham; o 1914 by Lyric Pictures Ltd; s 2,000; c 1918; sold to YMCA for theatre use; damaged by fire 21.3.53; rebuilt; cd 1960.

MAJESTIC 110 Smith Street (30 Inglefield St); Govanhill; o 7.12 by Arthur Vivian's Pictures Ltd; a Albert V. Gardner; s 959; sold to H.

Maitles 3.40; cd 1957.

MARNE 25 Marne Street; Dennistoun; o 16.11.20 by Eastern Picture House Co; a Duff and Cairns; s 1,300; renamed Park Cinema 5.28; cd 6.58.

MARYHILL PICTURE HOUSE 1397 Maryhill Road; Maryhill; o 12.14 by Maryhill Picture House Ltd; a George N. Beattie; s 830; cd 1929.

MAXWELL PICTURE HOUSE 99–107 Shawbridge St; Pollockshaws; o 4.21 by James Graham; a J. Jeffrey Waddell; s 980; leased to Bernard Frutin 8.32; renamed Palladium; sold to J. Boe; c 6.34; sold to James Graham; sold to Miss A. Burns 4.45; renamed Pollock Picture House; s 800; cd 9.58.

MAYFAIR 33 Sinclair Drive; Battlefield; o 22.1.34 by Mayfair Pictures Ltd; a Eric A. Sutherland; s 1,340; sold to ABC 9.35; c 30.6.73; wa rehouse; d 1980.

MECCA Balmore Road; Possil; o 16.8.33 by George Smith and James Welsh; a James McKissack; s 1,620; sold to Singleton Cinemas Ltd 7.1.50; renamed Vogue; c 4.68; bingo.

MOSSPARK PICTURE HOUSE Paisley Road West; Mosspark; o 1925 by Duncan Campbell; a John Caldwell (builders); s 1,000, sold 1938 to Scottish Central Cinemas (CAC); cd 24.11.73.

NEW BEDFORD 117 Eglinton Street; Laurieston; o 1921 by Bedford Picture House Ltd; sold to Bernard Frutin 7.24; destroyed by fire 3.32; demolished.

NEW BEDFORD 117 Eglinton Street; Laurieston; o 31.12.32 by Bernard Frutin; a Lennox and McMath; s 2,300; sold to George Green Ltd 1936; c 8.7.73; bingo.

NEW GRAND 118 Cowcaddens Street; Cowcaddens; o 1.4.19 on site of Grand Theatre by Grand Theatre (Glasgow) Ltd; a George A. Boswell; s 1,775; renovated 1926; s 1,768; leased to Grove Picture House Ltd from 1933; sold 1936 to same; closed 3.59; d 1966.

NEW KENT 11–15 Kent Road; Anderston; o 1921 by M.S. Lipton; s 910; sold 7.25 to New Kinema (Springburn) Ltd; c 5.31; garage.

NEW SAVOY Hope Street; City Centre; o 16.12.11 as Savoy Music Hall; a James Miller; sold to Biocolour Circuit 25.12.16; renamed New Savoy; s 2,000; sold to Gaumont 1927; c 12.9.58; converted to Majestic Ballroom; cd 15.1.72.

NEW STAR 1046 Maryhill Road; Maryhill; o 31.12.12 by Maryhill

Star Palace Ltd; Albert V. Gardner; s 900; rebuilt 1930; a Gardner; s 1,799; c 10.66; car showroom; d 1978.

NORWOOD 101 St Georges Road; Woodlands; o 6.36 by A.E. Pickard; a Laird and Napier; s 1,200; sold 1945 to Associated G.P. Cinemas; sold 4.5.58 to ABC; c 20.9.75; renamed Dreamland to show Asian films; c 1981; snooker club.

OLYMPIA 4 Orr Street; Bridgeton; o 18.9.11 as Olympia Theatre of Varieties; a George Arthur and Frank Matcham; s 2,000; sold 1924 to Scottish Cinema and Variety Theatres; rebuilt and reopened 21.11.38; a Charles J. McNair and Elder; s 1,689; renamed ABC 1963; c 9.3.74; bingo from 1987.

ORIENT 571 Gallowgate; Bridgeton; o 2.5.32 by George Taylor; a Albert V. Gardner; s 2,570; sold to George Green Ltd 1959; c 26.5.65; bingo; c 8.95; derelict.

OXFORD PLAYHOUSE 57 Keppochhill Road; Springburn; o 1927 by Bernard Frutin; a Lennox and McMath; s 1,500; destroyed by fire 1.1.41; d.

PALACE 129 Main Street (Gorbals St); Gorbals; o 1904 by Harry McKelvie; a Bertie Crewe; s 2,000; cine-variety from 1914; sold to H. Maitles 1.30; c 1962; bingo; cd 1976.

PALACEUM 10 Hill Street (Edrom St); Shettleston; o 1913 by George Urie Scott; a Charles J. McNair; s 835; rebuilt 1936; a McNair; damaged by fire; cd 9.54.

PALADIUM 1289 Dumbarton Road; Scotstoun; o 1910 by Scotstoun Paladium Ltd; a Brand and Lithgow; s 480; cd 1924.

PANOPTICON 115 Trongate; City Centre; o 1857 as Britannia Music Hall within Trongate House; sold 1899 to A.E. Pickard; rebuilt as Panopticon; a Bildard and McFarlane; cine-variety from 1910; renamed Tron Cinema 3.22; renamed Panopticon 8.27; c 7.38; stalls converted to shop; amusement arcade.

PARADE 490 Alexandra Parade; Dennistoun; o 3.8.10 by George Smith and James Welsh; s 350; c 2.21; derelict.

PARADE 200 Meadowpark Street; Dennistoun; o 14.2.21 by George Smith and James Welsh; a Stoddart and Paterson; s 1,436; sold to Gaumont 1928; c 3.8.61; bingo; reopened as New Parade Cinema 30.6.69 by Minor Bingo Entertainments; c 7.4.86; derlict; pub from 1993.

PARAGON 403 Cumberland Street; Gorbals; o 1912 by Cumberland

Picture House Ltd; s 1,300; sold 11.12 to R.V. Singleton; rebuilt 1927; a Albert V. Gardner and William R. Glen; sold to Odeon 9.36; cd 6.58.

PARAGON Tobago Street; Bridgeton; former Globe Music Hall; o 1910 by R.V. Singleton; s 683; cd 1920.

PARAMOUNT Renfield Street; City Centre; o 31.12.34 by Paramount (Glasgow) Ltd; a Frank T. Verity and Samuel Beverly; s 2,748; sold to Odeon 1939; tripled 2.10.70; a Dry, Halasz Dixon Partnership; s 1,138, 1,229, 558; screens 2 and 3 subdivided 4.86 to form six screen multiplex; s 1,138, 210, 230, 243, 288, 222.

PARKHEAD PICTURE PALACE 49 Tollcross Road; Parkhead; o 7.21 by Scottish Cinema and Variety Theatres; a George Gunn; s 1,250; cd 19.8.60.

PARTICK PICTURE HOUSE 14 Vine Street (Orchard St); Partick; o 4.11.12 by Partick Picture House Ltd (George Taylor); a Albert V. Gardner; s 1,295; rebuilt 1919; a Gardner; destroyed by fire 8.29; rebuilt and reopened 1.31; a Gardner; s 1,815; destroyed by fire 1962; rebuilt as warehouse; d 1982.

PHOENIX Sawfield Place; Woodside; o 1921 by Northern Kinema Ltd; a D MacNaughton and Son; s 980; sold to ABC 9.28; sold to K.M. Dunn 1943; renamed Endrick 23.12.48; c 9.55; warehouse; d 1972.

THE PICTURE HOUSE Sauchiehall Street; City Centre; o 19.12.10 by PCT; a Naylor and Sayle; s 1,140; rebuilt and reopened 18.12.12; a Naylor and Sayle; s 1,600; foyer rebuilt 7.24; a P.L. Browne; sold to Gaumont 23.3.29; renamed Gaumont 6.47; cd 15.1.72; Savoy Centre; listed frontage.

PLAZA 727 Govan Road; Govan; o 21.12.36 by ABC; a Charles J. McNair and Elder; s 2,280; renamed ABC 1966; c 15.4.72; d 10.72.

POSSILPARK PICTURE HOUSE 277 Saracen Street; Possil; o 1920 by James Graham; a Albert V. Gardner; s 1,282; sold 4.4.45 to Glasgow and West of Scotland Cinemas; s 1,222; sold to CMA (Rank) 23.4.55; cd 1960.

PREMIER 1138 Dumbarton Road; Scotstoun; o 1922; c 1930.

PREMIER 903 Shettleston Road; Shettleston; o 8.12 by George Urie Scott; s 432; c 1948; social club.

PRINCES 20 Gourlay Street; Springburn; o 9.14 by Scottish Picture House Ltd; a Richard Henderson; s 998; sold to Scottish Cinema and Variety Theatres 1917; cd 1936.

PRINCES 20 Gourlay Street; Springburn; o 8.11.37 by ABC; a Charles J. McNair and Elder; s 2,050; c 27.7.68; bingo; d 1979.

PRINGLE'S BIJOU HALL 73 Cowcaddens Street; Cowcaddens; o 19.3.08 by Ralph Pringle; s 650; cd 1930.

PRINGLE'S DENNISTOUN PALLADIUM Hillfoot Street; Dennistoun; o 1.1.12 by Ralph Pringle; a George A. Boswell; s 1,200; c 12.21; dance hall; d 1937.

PRINGLE'S PICTURE PALACE 12 Watson Street; Calton; former Queen's Theatre; o 11.11.07 by Ralph Pringle; s 1,200; c 7.14; reverted to theatre and renamed Queen's Theatre; leased to Bernard Frutin; cine-variety until 7.34; vaudeville until destroyed by fire in 1952; d 1956.

QUEEN'S CINEMA 160 Battlefield Road; Langside; o 1922 by Battlefield Pictures Ltd; a Albert V. Gardner; s 550; sold to R. Pennycook 6.34; renamed Tonic; sold to Loray Circuit 11.1.55.; c 1962; shop.

REGAL 326 Sauchiehall Street; City Centre; o 1875 as the Diorama; rebuilt 1888 as The Panorama; rebuilt 1885 as Ice Skating Palace; cinema shows from 26.5.1896; rebuilt as The Hippodrome 1904; became Hengler's Circus from 1904; rebuilt as Waldorf Palais de Danse 1927; o 13.11.29 as Regal by ABC; a Charles J. McNair; s 2,359; renamed ABC Regal 9.59; renamed ABC 1 19.10.67; quadrupled and reopened 3.12.79; a Howard and Unick; s 970, 306, 206, 192; renamed Cannon 5.86; damaged by fire 10.92; renovated and renamed MGM Cinemas 18.12.92.

REX 650 Cumbernauld Road; Riddrie; o 7.12.31 by ABC; a Charles J. McNair; s 2,336; renamed ABC 1961; cd 29.9.73.

RHUL Stonelaw Road; Burnside; o 27.4.32 by Burnside Picture House Co Ltd; a Neil C Duff; s 1,250; sold to ABC 12.36; cd 5.11.60.

RIDDRIE 726 Cumbernauld Road; Riddrie; o 20.3.38 by George Smith and James Welsh; a James McKissack; s 1,750; sold to Singleton Cinemas Ltd 7.1.50; renamed Vogue; c 4.68; bingo.

RIO Canniesburn Toll; Bearsden; o 8.10.34 by Suburban Pictures Ltd; a Cowiesons Ltd (builders); s 1,120; sold to Peter Crerar 6.36; sold to Scottish Central Cinemas (CAC) 6.38; twinned 1975; s 229, 287; cd 18.10.86.

RIO Glasgow Road; Rutherglen; o 23.9.35 by Suburban Pictures Ltd; a Cowiesons (builders); s 2,017; sold to Peter Crerar 5.36; sold to Scottish Central Cinemas (CAC) 6.38; cd 1971.

ROSEVALE 467 Dumbarton Road; Partick; o 1920 by Rosevale Cinema Co; a Duff and Cairns; s 1,894; rebuilt 1932; s 2,100; c 1965; bingo until 1981; snooker until 1993; supermarket.

ROXY 1397 Maryhill Road; Maryhill; o 15.9.30 by James Graham; a Lennox and McMath; s 2,270; sold 4.4.45 to Glasgow and West of Scotland Cinemas Ltd; sold to CMA (Rank) 23.4.55; cd 15.10.62.

ROYAL 102 Main Street; Bridgeton; o 7.18 by Royal Picture House Co; s 500; cd 3.58.

SALON 90 Sauchiehall Street; City Centre; o 6.13 by The Picture Salon Ltd; a Thomas Baird Jnr; s 950; superdrug, restaurant and disco.

SCENIC PICTURE HOUSE 457 Paisley Road West; Kinning Park; o 3.11.10 by Paisley Road Electric Palace Co Ltd; a Albert V. Gardner; s 800; cd 1938.

SCOTIA 7 Millerston Street; Bridgeton; o 24.3.21 by James Hamilton; a Charles J. McNair; s 1,250; sold to The Douglas Picture House Co 11.45; damaged by fire 17.2.49; rebuilt; c 1964; bingo until 1985; d 1987.

SCOTT'S ANNFIELD ELECTRIC THEATRE Gallowgate; Parkhead; o 1909 by George Urie Scott; s 600; c 4.34.

SCOTT'S ELECTRIC THEATRE Gray Street; Shettleston; o 3.12 by George Urie Scott; s 700; cd 5.20.

SEAMORE 220 Maryhill Road; Maryhill; o 21.12.14 by A.E. Pickard; a George A. Boswell and R.A. Thomas; s 1,942; rebuilt 1926; a H. Barnes; sold to A.B. King 4.35.; sold to CMA (Rank) 23.4.55; c 1963; destroyed by fire 1968; d 1968.

SHAWLANDS PICTURE HOUSE 1045 Pollokshaws Road; Shawlands; o 1914 by Shawlands Cinema Ltd; a Richard Henderson; s 550; sold to Scottish Cinema and Variety Theatres 4.16; cd 30.8.30.

SPRINGBURN ELECTRIC THEATRE 339 Springburn Road; Springburn; o 1911 by Caledonian Cinematograph Co Ltd; a Neil C. Duff; s 500; renamed Ideal Picture House 7.16; renamed Royal 2.25; c 1930; billiard hall; bingo from 1961; d 1979.

SPRINGBURN PICTURE HOUSE Wellfield Street; Springburn; o 1920 by James Graham; a Albert V. Gardner; s 1,535; sold 4.4.45 to Glasgow and West of Scotland Cinemas Ltd; renamed Astor 11.47; sold to CMA (Rank) 23.4.55; c 17.11.66; destroyed by fire; d 1968.

STANDARD 95 Dumbarton Road; Partick; o 1909 by James

Graham; a Albert V. Gardner; s 1,153; sold 4.4.45 to Glasgow and West of Scotland Cinemas; cd 1957.

STAR 254 Garscube Road; Woodside; o 1912 by North Glasgow Theatre Ltd; renamed Cosmo 7.31; cd 9.33.

STAR PALACE 203 Dumbarton Road; Partick; o 2.10 by Star Animated Pictures; s 1,005; rebuilt 9.14; a Charles J. McNair; sold to Star Palaces Ltd and rebuilt 1920; a William Reid; c 7.25; rebuilt as Fyfe and Fyfe Palais de Danse; bingo.

STAR PALACE 136 Main Street; Bridgeton; o 1908 by Mrs M Laird; a J. and J. Laird; s 1,013; cd 1930.

STATE 293 Castlemilk Road; King's Park; o 20.12.37 by Cathcart Picture Playhouse; a Charles J. McNair and Elder; s 1,600; sold 6.71 to County Properties and Developments Ltd; renamed County; bingo from 1972.

STATE 1311 Shettleston Road; Shettleston; o 14.5.37 by Cathcart Picture Playhouse; a Charles J. McNair; s 2,009; from 1955 s 1149; c 4.5.73; derelict; d 1986. Halfords.

ST ENOCH PICTURE THEATRE Argyle Street; City Centre; o 1881 as Crouch's Theatre of Varieties (later known as Crouch's Wonderland); films first shown in 1897; rebuilt and reopened 7.1.13 as St Enoch Picture Theatre by St Enoch Pictures Ltd; a George A. Boswell; s 600; c 1935; Dolcis shoe shop.

ST JAMES' PICTURE HOUSE 112 Stirling Street; Townhead; o 1910 by The Douglas Picture House Co; s 450; cd 1947.

STRATHCLYDE 41 Summerfield Street; Dalmarnock; o 15.8.28 by Strathclyde Cinema Ltd; a Albert V. Gardner and William R. Glen; s 1,910; sold to George Green Ltd 1937; c 7.5.61; bingo from 1962; d 1980.

SUN PICTURE PALACE Hopehill Road; Woodside; o 1911 by Leone Weinstone; a Bruce and Hay; cd 1914.

TEMPLE 80 Fulton Street; Anniesland; o 1917 by A. Wardrop; s 464; c 1924; workshop; d 1985.

THEATRE DE LUXE 417 Sauchiehall Street; City Centre; o 16.11.11 by De Luxe Theatre Co; a Albert V. Gardner; s 262; c 1930; restaurant.

THE TIVOLI 53 Crow Road; Partick; o 29.4.29 by Thomas Ormiston; a Denny and Blain; s 1,915; sold to Gaumont 3.32; sold to Classic 12.67; renamed Classic; c 26.2.72; bingo.

TOLEDO 380 Clarkston Road; Muirend; o 2.10.33 by Toledo Picture House Co; a William Beresford Inglis; sold 1,598; s to ABC 7.10.34; renamed ABC 20.7.70; tripled 25.2.82; a Howard and Unick; s 408, 208, 92; screen 3 closed 1.88; renamed Cannon 1986; listed building.

TUDOR Fenwick Road; Giffnock; o 12.36 by Crescent Cinema Co (Bernard Frutin); a Lennox and McMath; s 2,400; cd 8.62.

VAUDEVILLE PICTURE HOUSE 28 Argyle Street; City Centre; o 7.14; a Albert V. Gardner; c 1923; shop.

VITAGRAPH 520 Sauchiehall Street; City Centre; o 1912 by Vitagraph Picture Theatre Ltd; a John Fairweather; s 625; renamed King's 12.14; sold to Scottish Cinema and Variety Theatres 1917; renovated and reopened 24.9.31; c 4.1.54; sold to Capital and Provincial News Theatres; renamed Newscine; s 450; renamed Newcine 14.2.55; renamed Curzon 3.60; sold to Classic 9.64; renamed Curzon Classic; renamed Tatler Cinema Club 29.7.73; renamed Curzon 3.81; c 22.2.84; derelict.

VOGUE 251 Langlands Road, Govan; o 4.7.38 by Singleton Cinemas Ltd; a James McKissack; s 2,500; c 30.12.61; bingo; cd 6.85.

VOGUE Main Street; Rutherglen; o 29.1.36 by Singleton Cinemas Ltd; a James McKissack; s 1,750; sold to Odeon 9.36; renamed Odeon; c 12.10.74; bingo.

WAVERLEY 18 Moss-side Road; Shawlands; o 25.12.22 by Shawlands Picture House Ltd; a Watson, Salmond and Gray; s 1,320; sold to ABC 9.29; renamed ABC 1964; c 31.3.73; bingo; snooker from 1982; listed building.

WELLINGTON PALACE 11 Commercial Road; Gorbals; o 1874 as Wellington Palace Music Hall; sold to J.J. Bennell and reopened 30.11.08; sold to R. Pennycook and rebuilt 1928; a Albert V Gardner; s 1,967; cd 5.57.

WEST END ELECTRIC THEATRE Sauchiehall Street; Anderston; o 1910 by West End Kinema Ltd; s c.250; c 1913.

WESTWAY 1754 Paisley Road West; Cardonald; o 8.4.35 by George Smith and James Welsh; a Bryden, Robertson and Boyd; s 1,400; sold to Singleton Cinemas Ltd 7.1.50; c 3.2.59; rebuilt as Flamingo Ballroom; bingo from 1974.

WHITE ELEPHANT 42 Kilmarnock Road; Shawlands; o 1927 by A.E. Pickard; a H. Barnes; s 1,900; sold 1934 to A.B. King; renamed

Elephant; c 1960; shops.

WHITEVALE THEATRE 845 Gallowgate; Bridgeton; o 1908 by George Green Ltd; s 660; cd 1929.

ZOO ELECTRIC THEATRE New City Road; Cowcaddens; o 31.1.11 by E.H. Bostock; a John Nisbet; s 420; c 4.9.11; reopened 4.12.11 as Joytown Grand Electric Theatre; c 10.18; supermarket, Chinatown and snooker club.

Bibliography

BOOKS

Atwell, D. *Cathedrals of the Movies*, Architectural Press, London, 1981.

Barnes, J. *The Rise of the Cinema in Great Britain*, Bishopgate Press, London, 1983.

Cunnison, J. and Gilfillan, J.B.S. *The Third Statistical Account of Scotland: Vol. V Glasgow*, Collins, Glasgow, 1994.

Eyles, A. *ABC – The First Name in Entertainment*, British Film Institute, London, 1994.

Low, R. *A History of the British Film 1906–1914*, Allen and Unwin, London, 1949.

McKean, C. *The Scottish Thirties*, Scottish Academic Press, Edinburgh, 1987.

McLaren Young, A. and Doak, A.M. (Eds) *Glasgow at a Glance*, Collins, Glasgow, 1965.

Morton, H. *A Hillhead Album*, Hepburn Trust, Glasgow 1973.

Oakley, C.A. *Fifty Years at the Pictures*, Scottish Film Council of the BFI, Glasgow, 1946.

Stuart, A. *You Must Remember This . . . The Story of Springburn's Cinemas*, Springburn Museum Trust, Glasgow, 1990.

PERIODICALS

The Architect's Journal
Building Industries/The Builder
Educational Film Bulletin (September 1946)
The Kinematograph Year Book (1915-1972)
Milden Miscellany (1949)
Picture House (No.12, 'With ABC in Scotland' by G. Coombes)
Scottish Architect and Builder's Journal
Scottish Country Life (SMT Magazine)
Scottish Entertainer and Kinema Weekly

Index